The Mikoyan-Gur

MiG-1 & MiG-3
In Profile & Scale

Erik Pilawskii

Contents

RED BANNER
AVIATION
RESEARCH · ARTWORK · PUBLICATION

www.redbanner.co.uk

First Published 2011
ISBN 978-0-244-33089-7
Fourth Edition

MiG-1 and MiG-3

'MiG' – the terse acronym formed by the combination of the initials of two Soviet aeronautical engineers Artem Mikoyan and Mikhail Gurevich (*Mikoyan i Gurevich*) has stood as a popular moniker for Soviet jet fighters for six decades, and survives as a household word to this day. Extraordinarily, the first of a long line of otherwise successful fighters emanating from their joint Bureau was designed by neither Mikoyan nor Gurevich, was not a particular success, and represented the sort of political machination, intrigue, and manoeuvring worthy of a modern investigative documentary. The small, rakish, long-nosed I-200 was remarkable not only for the speed of its development, but also for the speed of its withdrawal from manufacture and the consequent fall from grace of several leading figures in the Soviet Aviation Industry.

The MiG programme was a classic case of governmental interference in industry; of panicked manufacture under duress; of ego, politicking and determination. And yet, for all that, the aircraft served the nation at a time of maximum peril, and wrote a glorious chapter in the annals of aerial warfare during the defence of Moscow in 1941.

The fascinating history of the I-200 and its development is not the subject of this volume, however. Readers are advised to look to other works, such as the author's *Soviet Air Force Fighter Colours* (Ian Allen, 2003), for such details. In this Profile and Scale series we will examine the visual record of the aircraft, demonstrating many individual examples through artwork, and by presenting scale line drawings of the various versions. The arrangement of these graphical elements is mainly chronological, according to the appearance of the different versions of the MiG fighter.

The primary line drawings presented in this work are completed in 1:48 scale, which is common for many modellers. Detail and exploded views are scaled variously, as indicated. Notation and photographic examples have been provided to assist the modeller and historian to detect the various differences between the versions, and also amongst permutations in manufacture. These drawings are the result, it must be added, of very many years' strenuous labour, and at the time of writing certainly may be entertained as the most accurate-- and hopefully complete-- of their type anywhere.

Here, then, is the MiG fighter family: *in Profile and Scale*.

The I-200 Prototypes

The I-200 no.1 prototype at Moscow, April 1940. The finish looked to have been over-all white with a red cheat-line. White painted prototypes were a Polikarpov OKB speciality, and this machine seemed to be similar, perhaps highlighting indeed the role of the great designer in the creation of the I-200 concept.

The no.3 prototype whilst under examination by the NII VVS, August 1940. The hinged canopy-- so utterly detested by Soviet pilots-- had been removed in fear that the aircraft would fail its State tests on that very grounds. The machine was finished in glossy AEh-15 Green lacquer-- a Factory 39 trade-mark-- with A2 Blue undersurfaces. The lower colour demarcation on the rudder was quite odd, but seen on more than one MiG built at this facility.

This mysterious looking early MiG is thought to be the *Izdeliya 61* (a.k.a. no.4) prototype, which formed the basis of MiG-3 manu-facture. The classic Factory 39 finish is evident, complete with rudder demarcation. The aircraft sports MiG-3 type cowling details, sliding canopy, 6 ° wing dihedral and armament, yet appears to be fitted with a small radiator. The appearance may be compared to the no.3 prototype just above.

The Series MiG-1

Only 100 MiG-1s were ever delivered, and many of these were beset with technical and manufacturing difficulties of every description. As a result, the number of such aircraft in service at the time of the *Barbarossa* invasion must have been quite modest. Images of *bona fide* MiG-1s, therefore, are exceptionally rare. This example is likely the best known to us in the photographic record and was captured in a wrecked condition by German forces, date unknown (but presumably during 1941). The angle of the photo makes the identification of the tactical number difficult; on balance it seems most likely to have been "6", though "8" and "3" could have been a possibility as well. "White 6" did not feature a radio mast, and the canopy was clearly in view [some early MiGs had the canopy removed]. The finish was an over-all "non-camouflage" application of A2 Green with A2 Blue undersurfaces, and national star insignia were carried on the wing upper surfaces.

One aircraft available on June 22, 1941, which has been persistently claimed to be a MiG-1 is this example, "White 2". This machine was the personal mount of V.N. Buyanov (later HSU) of the 146 IAP, Bryansk Front. The available photograph depicting this specimen is poor in the extreme, and this profile must therefore be regarded as a speculative reconstruction of the original appearance. The tactical number "2" is in view and appears to have been applied at a 'ground angle', and there *seems* to be a national star present on the fin/rudder; no details of the fuselage are in view. What is clear, however, is the early style Factory 39 type finish of AEh-15 Green with the curious lower colour demarcation extending to the rudder, a fact which does indeed suggest a MiG-1 version. Many examples of MiG-1s were distributed to the 146 IAP at Evpretoria before the war, and it is quite plausible to speculate that this example might have remained in service for a short while.

The Early MiG-3

This well published image presents an outstanding portrait of the very early MiG-3 Production Number (*p/n*) 2171. All of the hall-marks of the earliest MiG-3s are in view, including the "Yak" type exhaust fairing, short radio mast positioned aft, and other sundry details. The tactical number "1" was unusually trimmed with a green-blue paint which is thought to be the ubiquitous *Metal-Use Primer*. The non-camouflage finish was typical for early MiG manufacture, save for the use of black bordered stars on the fuselage and wing. The remains of "Red 1" are still preserved in the *Ilmailumuseo* collection, Finland.

[Below] "Red 12" was another early MiG-3 from the p/n 2100-2300 block, and exhibited similar details to "Red 1", above. The aircraft appears to have been little used in the photograph, and was certainly captured before seeing much action. Many early MiGs were abandoned in this way during the disastrous retreats of the summer of 1941. Note the considerable wear to the paint along the port side wing root-- quite typical for A2 lacquer when applied to un-primed metal surfaces.

This aircraft is thought to be the very early MiG-3 p/n 2115, as seen outside of the factory in Moscow. P/N 2115 was partly re-built at Factory 39, and then subjected to various facility tests throughout February 1941, seeking to rectify all manner of production shortcomings. The curious Factory 39 AEh-15 scheme and rudder colour demarcation are evident here. "White 15" carried national star insignia on the wing upper and lower surfaces, and smaller such markings on the fuselage, but none of the fin/rudder.

[Above, Below] Another MiG which was photographed after having been captured by German forces, "Red 14" is a classic example of manufacture from the p/n 2300-2650 range. Various types of fittings are seen on this example, mounted in the threaded lugs in the lower wing surfaces, to accommodate all manner of crutches and munitions. This aircraft was, again, devoid of any serious wear, and one wonders if this example ever managed to take to the skies in anger?

Whilst being clear and relatively sharp, the image of MiG-3 "42" is frustratingly indeterminate. The film type used in the photograph is notoriously over-sensitive to red light, and thus the national stars take on a 'white-washed' like appearance. For this reason, the colour of the tactical numeral cannot be known-- it could conceivably be red or white. The aircraft was filmed in service with the 7 IAP on the Leningrad Front, 1941, and a degree of re-painting was evident along the lower rear fuselage demarcation line.

This aircraft is the subject of a well published photograph depicting a German soldier striking a pose of ironic "superiority" over the derelict *untermenschen* foe. The image reveals quite excellent details on the aircraft, again representative of manufacture in this range (2300-2650), and is equally valuable as a comparative tool with various other known aviation colours in view (as on the Ju 52 in background). The colour of the tactical number cannot be determined definitively (on such German film types), but on balance the appearance seems to agree best with the undersurface colour of A2 Blue. The gloss surface of the original AEh-15 finish is quite evident, as is the sensitivity of such film types to the amount of light reflected, which modifies the apparent tone of the colours on the image.

Despite its considerably disassembled state, "White 9" would appear on balance to be another example of this block of MiG-3s. The aircraft was seen wearing the remnants of a winter MK-7 White applique, some portions of which might well have been deliberately removed to affect a field type scheme. The national star on the fin/rudder is curious, and doubtless hand applied, harkening back to such insignia of the "Award Star" variety seen during the 1920s and 30s.

[Right] "White 9" shown here in a rather derelict condition, having been loaded onto a flat car for transport. Various labels and other devices seem to have been applied to the airframe, no doubt specifying the eventual destination and other instructions or manifests.

[Left] "White 3" shown abandoned and captured by German forces, 1941. Interesting fittings are seen under the starboard wing of this MiG. The finish here is classic for early machines in the pre-War (non-camouflage) style, and one suspects that national star insignia would have been seen on the wing upper surfaces.

"White 3" looks to have been an early MiG of the same p/n 2300-2650 block. The fin/rudder feature a nice bit a trim whose colour cannot be determined with any certainty; it here rendered in yellow, but all manner of other choices are equally possible.

The primary MiG-3 fighter built prior to the outbreak of war was in fact a five-gun model with under-wing BK gun-pods installed at the factory. However, of these a very significant proportion had their under-wing armament removed, as the deterioration in the aircraft's performance and handling was not appreciated by most pilots. "White 25" was typical of such MiGs in the p/n 2650-3400 range, and many such examples featured puttied or otherwise sealed over ammunition access hatches.

This delightful MiG shows the signs of very significant re-finishing, and similarly had its BK gun-pods removed. A gloss black paint was employed in these efforts-- likely AEh-11 Black-- giving a rather curious appearance. The VVS' penchant for having more than one tactical number in view was seen here, and one is at a loss to describe the machine as "40" or "6"; the latter of which, more curiously, appears to be yellow in colour. Rails typical of the MiG for six RS-82 missiles were installed, but these appear to have been painted similarly with AEh-11. The under-wing ammunition hatch appears to have been sealed and given identical treatment.

Some MiGs manufactured before June 1941 did retain their 5-gun arrangement in service, such as this example which was photographed after having crashed by German forces during October. The finish was a rather early type of non-camouflage application in A2 lacquers, but no national stars were seen on the wing upper surfaces. It is not clear if the small "81" on the rudder is the tactical number, or some kind of other notation.

[Above, Below] This rather used specimen presents a number of most fascinating curiosities to the careful observer. The aircraft is clearly from the p/n 2650-3400 block, and yet none of these were thought to have had wing leading edge slats fitted during manufacture. The outer wings here do have slats, and more than that, the starboard unit (at least) has been painted top and bottom with a fresh coat of MK-7 White. No national insignia is present on the lower surface, but six rails have been fitted for RS-82 rockets. One would speculate that the wing outer sections are replacements (or perhaps an upgrade), and not original, and that their curious painting is related to this fact. The rather large black-bordered star and unusual lower colour demarcation on the fuselage are notable, as is the tidy appearance of the aircraft's tail section and the national insignia placed there. No tactical number is in view.

The 401 and 402 IAPs

This aircraft demonstrated the curious and distinctive camouflage and tactical number font of the 401 and 402 IAPs during the defence of Moscow, late 1941. These schemes consisted of a single black band of colour on each wing and stabiliser upper surface, and a 'blob' of similar lacquer over the nose and fin/rudder. "White 43" did not sport the nose colour feature, but in all other respects was typical of these examples.

"White 42" of the 401 IAP is another classic example of these regiments' MiG-3s around Moscow. The tactical numeral in this case shows the more careful attention and skill usually noted on such examples, being rather well executed in their own handsome font style.

The 401 IAP, in particular, sometimes employed an 'alternate' distinctive font on aircraft wearing this pattern, as shown here on "White 57". This machine is another classic example of the p/n 2650-3400 range MiG-3, with its under-wing BK gun-pods having been removed in service.

This fascinating MiG-3 presents an exceptionally curious appearance. The field application of camouflage seems to have started very nicely on the forward cowling with typical VVS style semi-soft colour demarcations and a rounded pattern. This work was, for some reason, flagrantly interrupted and replaced by jagged, hard-edged applications of paint with no particular rationale in mind. The rudder is the strangest area in view, sporting a disastrously executed national star insignia, one which is incongruous with the neat part of the marking on the fin. A tactical numeral "0" remains on the fin, but a hand scribbled "10" may be found on the rudder. Over all, one wonders if the rudder was a replacement, hastily painted to restore what might originally have been "White 10"? We shall likely never know... The aircraft was an early cowling example of p/n 2650-3400 manufacture, but the wings appear to be fitted with leading edge slats, and the tail wheel has been replaced with a fixed unit. The extensive refurbishment of this machine might well have been completed at the regiment, quite probably explaining, in addition, the curious re-painting.

In Foreign Service

Although sporting certain incongruous and polyglot features-- as captured machines tend to do-- this example on balance seems to have been from the p/n 2650-3400 block of manufacture. The finish here in Romanian service is indeterminate; neither the film type nor relevant lacquers are known. The profile demonstrates re-finishing over the original A2 Green scheme with German RLM 71 paint and Axis pattern Eastern Front theatre markings. The numeral "2" and the code "E.19" are in white, whilst the application of the Romanian cross insignia to the wing undersurface is speculative.

Later Cowling MiG-3s

The somewhat deteriorated state of this image, combined with what must be a certain lack of attention to detail, has resulted in all manner of strange and fanciful mis-interpretations of "Red 02". The cowl pieces seem to exhibit slightly more wear-- or a slightly thinner application of MK-7 White-- than the fuselage, but nothing so dramatic as to suggest that these might be *unpainted*, for example [how these parts might be interpreted as unpainted dural sheet defies all understanding]. The stabiliser in view also exhibits this kind of thinned application, or perhaps removal of white paint (noting that the affected area extends onto the fairing). The colour of the wing upper surface is much debated, but in all respects its appearance best agrees in the image with the same red colour as found on the stars and tactical numeral. The suggestion that the wing outer panels are a replacement-- and therefore green in colour-- is without any basis: this aircraft was part of the p/n 3750-3850 batch and left the factory as seen here (e.g. without wing slats). Indeed, the pitot is still white in colour, except at the very base, which also in logical agreement with a red painted wing. Furthermore, the complaint that such a "gaudy" decoration would have been improbable is also erroneous-- aircraft displaying very large areas of red colour were commonly known throughout the whole of the Soviet VVS. MiGs, specifically, demonstrating painted outer wing panels are hardly unknown in the photographic record; the image here [Right] shows such another MiG-3 from the 12 IAP whose outer wings look to be painted red as on "02".

The national star insignia on "Red 02" were not carefully applied, being neither symmetrical nor particularly well aligned. Similarly, the upper/lower colour demarcation was curiously "low" with a strange 'ramp' feature aft. The spinner's colour is indeterminate, and here shown as black, while careful observation reveals that "02" was armed with RS-82 rockets, as were most of the machines in this often seen 120 IAP line-up.

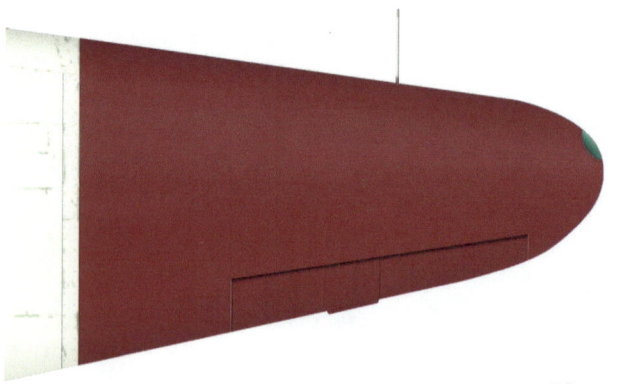

A personal favourite of the author, "Red 39" was certainly not painted on the most propitious day at the Regiment. The ad-hoc nature of the white applique was not uncommon, but the execution of the national star insignia was woeful to say the least. Equally, the tactical number "39" had been scribbled by hand, in fact so badly that the responsible party was not able even to complete it on a single side of the fin! Most of the aircraft in this line-up were armed with RS-82 rockets, which are shown here speculatively despite not being in view.

[Left] Part of the famous 120 IAP line-up featuring "Red 02", and other colourful MiGs. Little wonder that "39" has been placed in the centre of the group, likely in the hope that it would not have been noticed!

In rather stark contrast to "39", above, this attractive MiG-3 from the p/n 3850-4400 block shows a very much better (and artistic) finish. The national star insignia have been delightfully trimmed with a thin white border, perhaps prefacing in some ways the later modification to the VVS' markings. The camouflage pattern was certainly a field applique job, but in this case very professionally executed, and not at all dissimilar to certain factory patterns. The text along the fuselage spine reads, "*Death to the German Occupiers*", and was again completed in a very fine font style. The lower colour demarcation on the rear fuselage suggests that this aircraft was originally finished in a rather outdated single-colour (non-camouflage) A2 Green livery, which was a bit unusual for machines of this time frame built at Factory 1.

Another classic example of the p/n 3850-4400 range, "White 8" was armed with RS-82 rockets. The tactical numeral was quite unusually large and dramatically painted, whereas the camouflage looks to have been field applied in a tidy and professional manner. The machine was part of the 120 IAP as seen in August 1941.

"White 2" seems to have been an earlier example with the late pattern cowling, likely in the p/n 3400-3850 range (e.g. built without wing slats, etc). The photograph of this machine is too poor in quality to see if any stencil was present on the cowling, but six RS-82 rockets are in view. A small white flash was applied on the rudder tip, and the large tactical number "2" seems to have squeezed into the available space rather desperately. The aircraft appears in the same image as "White 8", above, and wears a notably similar field applied scheme.

"White 67" was photographed in flight over Leningrad during the winter of 1941-42. The identity of the unit to which this example belong is still a matter of considerable debate, but certainly the white spinners in view are reminiscent of certain Naval (VMF) regiments on that front. Be that as it may, the aircraft strikes a rather typical appearance for a MiG-3; note the slightly out-of-alignment national insignia.

This interesting example demonstrates a rather thinned application of MK-7 White lacquer, prefacing indeed the very same technique which would be commonly seen during the following winter when employing this finish. This application was made carefully over the temperate camouflage, edging around the national star insignia so as to avoid having to re-paint them. The aircraft was armed with RS-82 rockets and no tactical number can be seen.

[Left] Taxiing out, no doubt for another sortie. The tail wheel has received one of the numerous and popular modification to fix this item in the down position. Noting the ubiquity of this kind of work, presumably stuck and jammed tail gear were a problem in the MiG-3.

This famous MiG-3 is known from a widely published series of photographs taken by German personnel during 1941. Despite their popularity, the images are, in fact, very poor indeed, and much of the detail on the rear portion of this aircraft is hopelessly obscured. The colour profile here must, therefore, be regarded as a reconstructive attempt in these areas. The camouflage was certainly of a field applied type, with no information available on the rear lower colour demarcation area. It *may* be so that a rather crooked national star existed on the fin; analytical results are simply uncertain here due to the photograph's condition. The large inscription to port reads, "*For the Motherland*". No tactical number is in view.

Those persons who wish to "see" silver trim colouration everywhere on VVS aircraft do so with remarkable ease, despite the fact that no evidence *whatsoever* exists for such a practice. However, that said, this MiG-3 presents us with a very curious appearance which is quite difficult to explain. The quality of the photograph is indeed lacking, but what is clear is that the paint used for the tactical number is extremely gloss in finish; the amount of reflected light from its surface is striking. Few Soviet aviation lacquers exhibit this kind of gloss finish, and in this scenario lacquers AEh-15 Green and A2 Aluminium are the only real candidates to consider. Could the number have been a shiny dark green colour, or could it have been white (as usual) and the photograph manipulated or damaged? There are many possibilities, of course, but in this case "40" is shown with aluminium painted numerals. In other respects the aircraft is a later MiG-3 of the p/n 4400-4950 block, complete with an inert gas collection tube. Note the classic paint wear along the port wing root fairing.

"White 12" was another example of the later batch of MiG-3s as "40", above. This machine looks to be wearing a field applied scheme of slightly indifferent execution. The tactical number is quite attractive, with what must be described as a rather 'modern' looking font style. What was originally no doubt a nicely applied plain red star marking on the fin/rudder has been embellished with a clumsily and thickly applied white surround. The tail wheel has been modified with one of the classic fixed configurations so common on later MiGs.

16

This delightful MiG-3 was photographed at an unnamed flight school during the summer of 1943. As with many such machines, part of the school curriculum seems to have involved camouflaging the various aircraft; flight school examples being amongst the most colourful of all specimens across the entire pictorial record. "White 54" certainly does not disappoint in this respect. The rear fuselage seems to have been a replacement (again, typical of flight school equipment), making for a somewhat polyglot appearance. The dark and reflective surface suggests AEh-15 finish quite strongly, whilst the forward fuselage sports a freshly applied livery in three colours (here shown as A2 Black and Dark Green over Green). The spinner features a Hucks attachment and is delightfully painted (similar to the aircraft behind), while the tactical number has been very casually executed.

"Red 8" was an example of a rather beautifully turned out MiG-3 with a white winter finish which has, alas, been soiled by a considerable amount of exhaust staining (no doubt the result of an involved combat flight). The MK-7 finish was expertly applied, as were the tactical numeral and star national markings equally completed crisply. This machine looks certainly to have been manufactured in the p/n 3850-4400 block, and is a fairly classic example of later cowling pattern type MiGs. "Red 8" is reported to have belonged to V. Matkov of the 27 IAP, date unknown.

[Left, Above] One of a mere handful of MiG-3s which were stationed in the Far North, this example "White 57" served with the 147 IAP during early 1942. The aircraft is an earlier late cowling pattern machine without wing slats of the p/n 3400-3850 block. The very curious camouflage pattern was locally applied, featuring individual 'blobs' of colour on the wing upper surface, and further areas which do not reach over the top of the fuselage. The tactical number and spinner were white, and no indication of any under-wing armament is in view.

[Above, Below] "Red 90" served with the 12 IAP at Moscow during the winter of 1941-42. The winter finish seems to have been freshly applied and still in good condition. The aircraft looks to have been from the p/n 3400-3850 range, and featured an early form of fixed tail wheel modification. Six RS-82 rockets were carried. The trim, number and national markings were all executed in red; curiously, the lower right tip of the fuselage star markings has been cropped.

"Black 38" was another MiG-3 featuring in the famous series of photographs of the 120 IAP lined up in Moscow. This aircraft again demonstrates a varied and intriguing finish, with alternating areas of skill (or not) throughout. The winter application looks to have been worn, with considerable soot in view. The area of missing white finish is hard to explain; one wonders what might have led to such a pattern of removal? The outer wing under-surfaces and spinner have been painted with a fresh coat of MK-7 White, the latter also receiving a *spectacularly* executed star on its tip. White outer wing unders were something of a 'fad' in certain MiG equipped units, presumably in similar fashion-- and for the same reason, namely a large outer wing dihedral-- to the use of upper surface colours on the underside outer wings of Corsairs in the US Navy, for example.

"Black 12" was yet another white outer wing underside example from the 120 IAP line-up, Moscow. The combination of features in view-- particularly the presence of wing slats and the reduction gear ratio stencil to starboard-- help to identify this machine as one of the MiGs built in the last two weeks of July 1941. The pattern of wear in view is most curious, and for many years was thought to be a mere artefact of the damaged image. It now thought, however, that these areas are part of the actual appearance of "12", though one struggles to find a logical explanation for how such a pattern might develop. The rear lower colour demarcation was quite odd, perhaps explained by the tail wheel modification applied at the regiment. The national star insignia were again not impressively executed, particularly on the fin above the tactical numeral.

That MiG...

This iconic "photograph" of a MiG-3 roaring off the field is in fact a still taken from a roll of 16 mm *cine* film in the TASS archive dating from 1943. The quality of the image is poor to say the least, but one can identify this aircraft as a MiG-3 of the p/n 4400-4950 range, complete with inert gas collection tube and fixed tail wheel modification. The sliding canopy and radio mast have been removed, which is an uncommon sight on such late surviving MiGs. The spinner and tactical numeral were white in colour, the latter of which has been errantly drawn in many profile artworks by confusing its shape with a light reflection from the port wing tip. The camouflage is obviously some type of complex applique-- presumably over the original A2 Green livery-- but it is utterly beyond possibility to identify the pattern or overlying colours with certainty. The profile, above, represents this authors' best guess at the scheme using lacquers A2 Dark Green and Black, which seem to agree with the tonal properties of the image. Other possibilities using known aviation paints might include a combination of A2 Brown and Black, or even the later green finish AMT-4. No other useful details can be extracted from this frustrating and evocative image.

"White 27" showing an applique scheme using lacquers A2 Brown and A2 Black.

"White 27" showing an applique scheme using lacquers AMT-4 Green and A2 Black.

Black Sea MiGs

MiG-3s and P-40s lined up at the 7 IAP ChF VMF (Naval Black Sea Fleet), 1943.

"White 21" looks to be an example of the p/n 3850-4400 block of production, seen here still in service during 1943. The camouflage appears to remain mostly as originally applied, but the national star insignia have been embellished by very thick white borders of somewhat indifferent application. No under wing armament was present and the tail wheel has been replaced with a later style fixed modification. White, or white-and-red, spinners seemed to have been a squadron or regiment speciality, all of the machines in view being so decorated.

"White 28" is quite similar in many respects to "21" [above], resulting from the same batch of production and with the same fixed tail wheel modification. However, this aircraft features a *superbly* applied 'Kremlin' type national marking on the fin/rudder, again with a very thick white border. The font style used for these tactical numbers is very indicative of the 7 IAP ChF.

Seen towards the rear of the line up, "White 30" was not as especially handsome in appearance as the rest of these Naval MiGs in view. Although similar in configuration and age, the national stars and subsequent white borders have not been applied particularly well, resulting in a somewhat haphazard finish.

[Above, Below] "White 25", in the foreground, was a later MiG of the p/n 4950-5250 block of production with twin UBS armament. The larger fairings, missing intake scoops, and other details of this variant are clearly visible in this image. As with a number of such models, no inert gas tube is in view. The type of spinner fitted to this machine is also hidden, here shown as a normal (non-Hucks) type, whilst the tail wheel arrangement on this aircraft is similarly obscured.

"White 15" presents a rather typical appearance for a later cowl pattern MiG-3, albeit the font style of the tactical number is slightly odd. The camouflage looks to have been a known factory applied pattern with local 'touching up' around the cockpit. The date, location and unit of this aircraft are not currently known.

This aircraft is known from a well published image (another 16 mm still) showing MiG-3s in flight over Leningrad, 1941. RS rockets and a Hucks type spinner are in view, as is a typical Factory 1 camouflage application. The tail wheel seems to have been locked in the down position without any further modification (e.g. with gear doors open), surely which must have been a temporary and expedient fix for another malfunctioned unit.

[Right] "White 46" upper surface view.

Not all VVS pilots disliked the under wing BK gun pods, as demonstrated by this later MiG of the p/n 4400-4950 block. It is likely that none of these later examples were built with such armament at the Factory, but the 'universal' under wing fittings of the model allowed the gun pods to be added later if desired. "White 49" served with the 401 IAP, and its pilot must have preferred the extra hitting power of this arrangement (logical, noting that their primary targets were bombers) to the reduction in performance caused by them.

This long serving MiG-3 was photographed following some type of crash, with the cowling and spinner in considerable distress. The soft and variable nature of the applique camouflage is fascinating, and the colour in view has been vigorously debated as Dark Green or Black (here shown with the latter). The star on the fin/rudder was beautifully executed with a thin white border, but strangely in the outdated 1920s 'Awards Star' style. The tactical number "64" was not so carefully applied, and both it and the spinner were white in colour.

On balance, "Red 42" appears to be a twin UBS armed MiG of the p/n 4950-5250 group, and sported a particularly handsome winter application of MK-7 White. *Considerable* debate has followed as to whether this example may show an all-white MiG scheme-- finished with MK-7 on the upper *and* lower surfaces, both-- a few of which are known in the photographic record. The profile above presents this view, but that fact should not suggest that this particular debate has ended. A diminutive red star was painted on the tip of the spinner, and the national star insignia-- whilst well formed-- were not especially well aligned. The canopy had been removed, and no radio mast is in view.

Despite being the subject of a rather poor image, "White 5" presents us with the details of a quite extraordinary MiG-3. This aircraft was clearly a late example of the p/n 4950-5250 block armed with twin UBS guns and, as seen on some such models, no inert has collection tube is in view. However, under wing BK gun pods *are* in view, something which is certainly unique in the known photographic record. This combination would have imbued "5" with the relatively heavy armament (for a MiG-3, at least) of four 12.7 mm guns, and suggests further that not all Soviet pilots were averse to these extra weapons, despite their obvious weight and drag penalties. The finish, although quite similar to a classic Factory 1 camouflage application, was likely field applied, and the machine was fitted with a Hucks starter type spinner. Alas, no detailed information regarding the date nor owner of this unique specimen are available.

MiG-3 p/n 5077, "Black 2", was the personal mount of HSU E.M. Gorbatyuk, 28 IAP PVO. Gorbatyuk later served with the 63 GvIAP at Kursk, and subsequently became the regiment's commanding officer. He finished the war with 11 confirmed personal victories in 347 flights and remained in the Air Force, rising to Lt. General rank.

Given that the nose of p/n 5077 is not in view, this profile must be regarded as a speculative recreation of this area. However, from the machine's Production Number we do know that Gorbatyuk's "2" was a twin UBS armed example built during the third week of September 1941, and the remainder of the profile conveys details of such a model. The tactical number was originally applied to the rudder, but this was obliterated by the application of winter MK-7 finish (over temperate finish or as a touch up, one wonders?), whereas the p/n stencil has been faithfully retained on the fin. The 'new' numeral sports a decorative font style, dissimilar to the original, and again (it appears) in black. The fuselage national star marking, whilst well formed, has been applied at an inconceivably strange angle.

The Last Moscow MiGs

The winter of 1941-42 had been fraught with peril for Muscovites. Aerial bombing, indiscriminate artillery fire, food and fuel shortages all ensued as Fascist forces closed in on the capital. These troubles were exacerbated by the frantic efforts to relocate the various heavy industries and production facilities to the east, and to fortify Moscow against the invaders. By February 1942, German forces had been pushed back by Zhukov's winter counter-offensive, and the city, at last, could breath again. In this psychological and military thaw, routines of normal activity began to return.

So it was, thus, that at the old Factory No 1 complex the few remaining staff found several MiG parts and components left behind from the relocation to Kuibishev. Enough, indeed, to assemble three complete fighters. And so, with great pride, and not a little fanfare, the last MiG-3s built at Moscow were rolled out of the mostly empty production hall, all lovingly decorated with lighting bolts and dedication inscriptions. A fitting tribute, by all accounts, to an heroic manufacturing effort of the Great Patriotic War.

"For the Motherland" (*Za Rodinu*), the first of the line-up of these wonderful aircraft. Hand built, these machines were not exact specimens of the last parts of mass manufacture, but in most respects resembled the final series built at Moscow, with twin UBS armament and other refinements. The tail wheel was fixed, similarly to the later field modification of this type, and a single RO-132 rocket rail was installed under each wing. Interestingly, as well, the wing outer panels' undersurfaces were painted white, a practice seen often in the local MiG units around Moscow. The lower colour demarcation was executed quite low throughout, with a curious 'ramp' feature aft. *Za Rodinu* lacked a radio mast.

"For Stalin" (*Za Stalina*), the next machine in line. It is a matter of curiosity that of the three aircraft, this example's markings are the least professionally completed. Not only was the bolt/arrow feature more anaemic, but the national star insignia were poorly formed and aligned, both. A subtle political comment, one wonders, or mere coincidence? Though it is likely that all of these MiGs were so fitted, *Za Stalina* at least certainly sported an inert gas system, as evidenced by the starboard side view.

The last of these three lovely MiGs was this example, "For the Bol'shevik Party" (*Za Partiyu Bol'shevikov*). The national star insignia in this case were very finely executed, the fuselage marking being quite large. All of these aircraft were finished with a tidy coat of MK-7 White, and the usual A2 Blue undersurfaces. *Za Partiyu Bol'shevikov* was the only one of the three to sport a radio mast, but in all other respects seems to be similar to its neighbours. The bold red tipped spinners, bolt and other markings make for a stunning presentation and appearance.

"For the Bol'shevik Party" seen during the summer of 1942, now wearing a temperate field applied scheme. The original insignia and inscriptions were carefully retained, albeit the dedication text had been re-touched and thickened somewhat. The aircraft still has its RO132 rails, and also a new tail gear cover.

Recently Discovered Images

"White 97" was the recipient of some rather fanciful field appliqué camouflage. The various parts look to have been painted while the aircraft was in bits, and subsequently reassembled, giving a *helter-skelter* appearance. The tiny national star on the fin/rudder was not well applied, additionally, but may have been a remnant of the original finish, from which most of the paint over the windscreen and sliding canopy framing has fallen away. The aircraft was an example of the p/n 3400-3850 production block, but no under-wing armament options are in view (the outer wing is missing), and one cannot tell if a radio mast had been fitted.

This late series *2 x UBS* MiG (p/n 4950-5250) must have been finely turned out originally, and indeed still sports a fairly nice coat of MK-7 White. For reasons unknown, the fuselage star was disastrously altered, perhaps to accept the inscription "For Stalin!", which itself is nicely picked out over the national insignia. The nose and aft end of the fin/rudder are not in view, and those areas must be regarded as a speculative recreation here.

The MiG Family in Scale Line Drawings

The line drawings presented herein are entirely new, never before published. These represent the culmination of many years' labour, and are based where possible on direct measurements taken from pieces of existing examples. These drawings build on the excellent and popular work published by Voronin and Rodinov, based on the NKAP MiG-3 Maintenance Manual. As well, they are indebted the more recent but equally impressive efforts of Evgenniy Asen'ev, who has tirelessly uncovered the mysteries of the MiG programme, and issued quite outstanding scale plans of his own creation. Enormous credit must be assigned to Arsen'ev's work, without which a proper understanding of the MiG fighter would simply not be possible.

MiG fighters were assigned a Production Number (*p/n*) at the factory during manufacture. These p/n were allocated sequentially as the machines were built-- giving an approximate time frame for their completion-- and started, curiously, with the number 2000 (for the first MiG-1). These scale drawings are arranged by 'blocks' (or groups) of aircraft which were manufactured with similar features; ergo, roughly within the same time frame. Since modifications were often applied in a fluid manner, strict demarcations in production features were not usual. Therefore, it should not be understood that any given MiG variant started or ended precisely at the given p/n citation; these values are approximate, relating to the general time frame when a modification was introduced on the lines. The exception to this observation may be seen with the MiG-1, of which exactly 100 were manufactured, thus accounting for p/n 2000-2099; p/n 2100 was the first production MiG-3. To aide further in identifying the various groups of MiG-3s, the approximate dates for completion of the different versions is also given, for comparison.

All of the primary scale line drawings in this volume are presented in 1:48 scale. In cases where scrap or detail views are rendered in another scale, these will be noted directly on the drawing.

As with all scale line drawings, it is often the case that certain details are deliberately omitted from oblique views where such items would be either difficult to render, or might be misleading in a flat projection. This is so, often, as a result of the curvature or shape of the structure, leading to problems of representing such detail in a two-dimensional plane. The small rivets present on underwing panels or cowling seams when viewed from a side projection are examples of this kind of problem, and in these drawings have been omitted in those views. *As a result, readers are advised to consult the most perpendicular line drawing available for the definitive level of detail over any given area of the aircraft.*

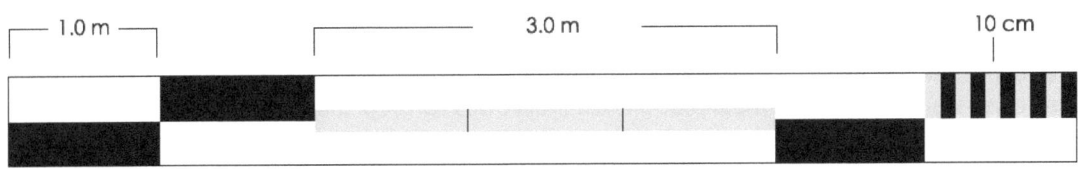

Special Line Drawing Features

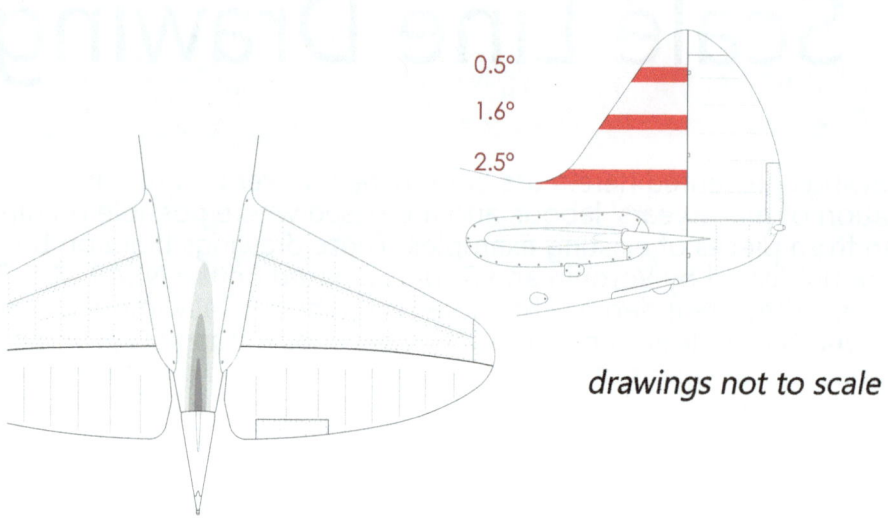

0.5°
1.6°
2.5°

drawings not to scale

All of the upper side views presented in this book feature a special three-colour shaded area around the aircraft's fin. The object of this shading is to clarify the *curvature* of the fin as it emerged from the rear fuselage. As the fin was built integrally with the fuselage, there are no panel lines or other devices by which one may differentiate the fin's exact position, and so this shading serves that role. The red highlighted areas (above right) show the approximate position of the "foot print" of this curvature as seen from above; that is to say that the base of the fin features a 2.5 degree deflection to starboard, whilst the middle section is closer to 1.6 degrees, and so on.

In no case should these shaded areas be confused with holes, apertures, or other surface details. These devices are provided as a guide to shape, only, and singularly exist on the upper surface drawings.

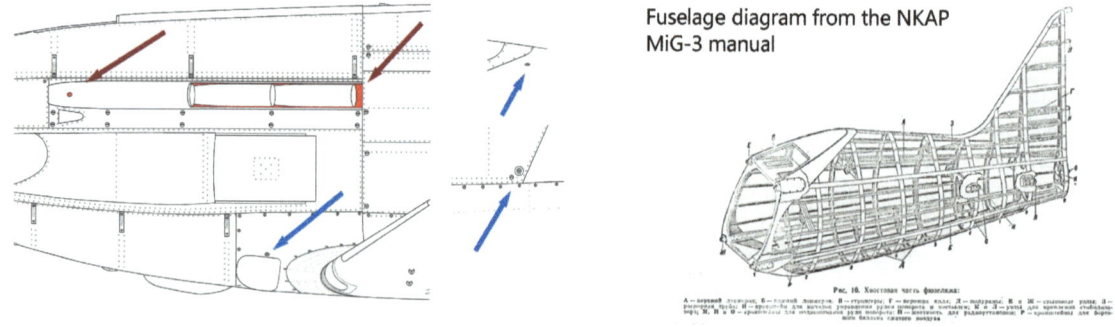

Fuselage diagram from the NKAP
MiG-3 manual

[Above, Left] Shading has been used in these line drawings to emphasize holes in the structure *where such details might be misinterpreted as surface features or panel lines* [blue arrows]. In cases where it was felt that the detail would clearly represent a hole feature [red arrows], no shading was employed. The intention was to keep such artistic 'artefacts' to a minimum so as to emphasize the line detail.

MiG-1 P/N 2000-2099

(completed ~ October - November 1940)

Armament:

2 x 7.62 mm synchronised ShKAS mounted above engine
each with 750 cartridges

1 x 12.7 mm synchronised UBS mounted above engine with 300 cartridges

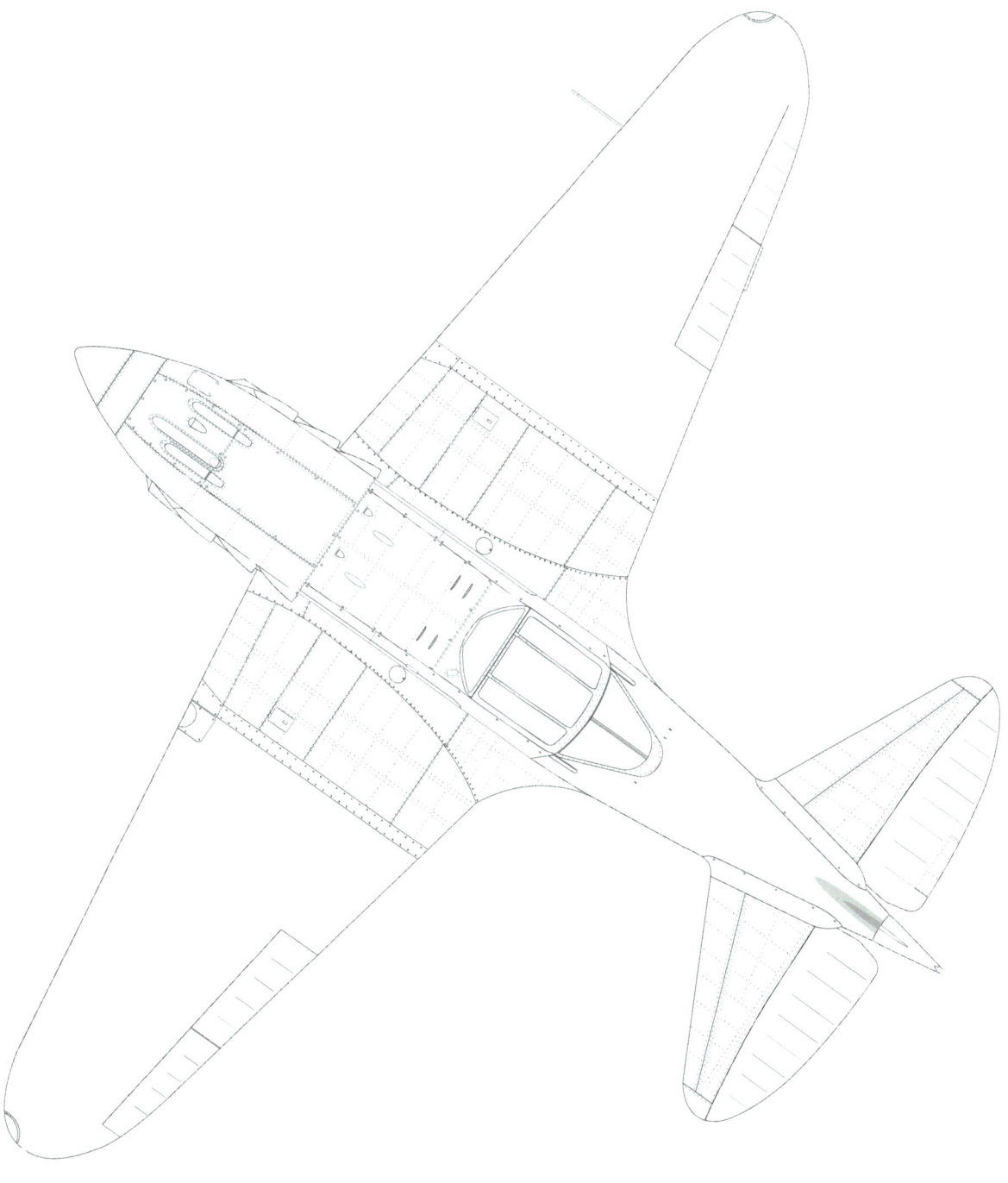

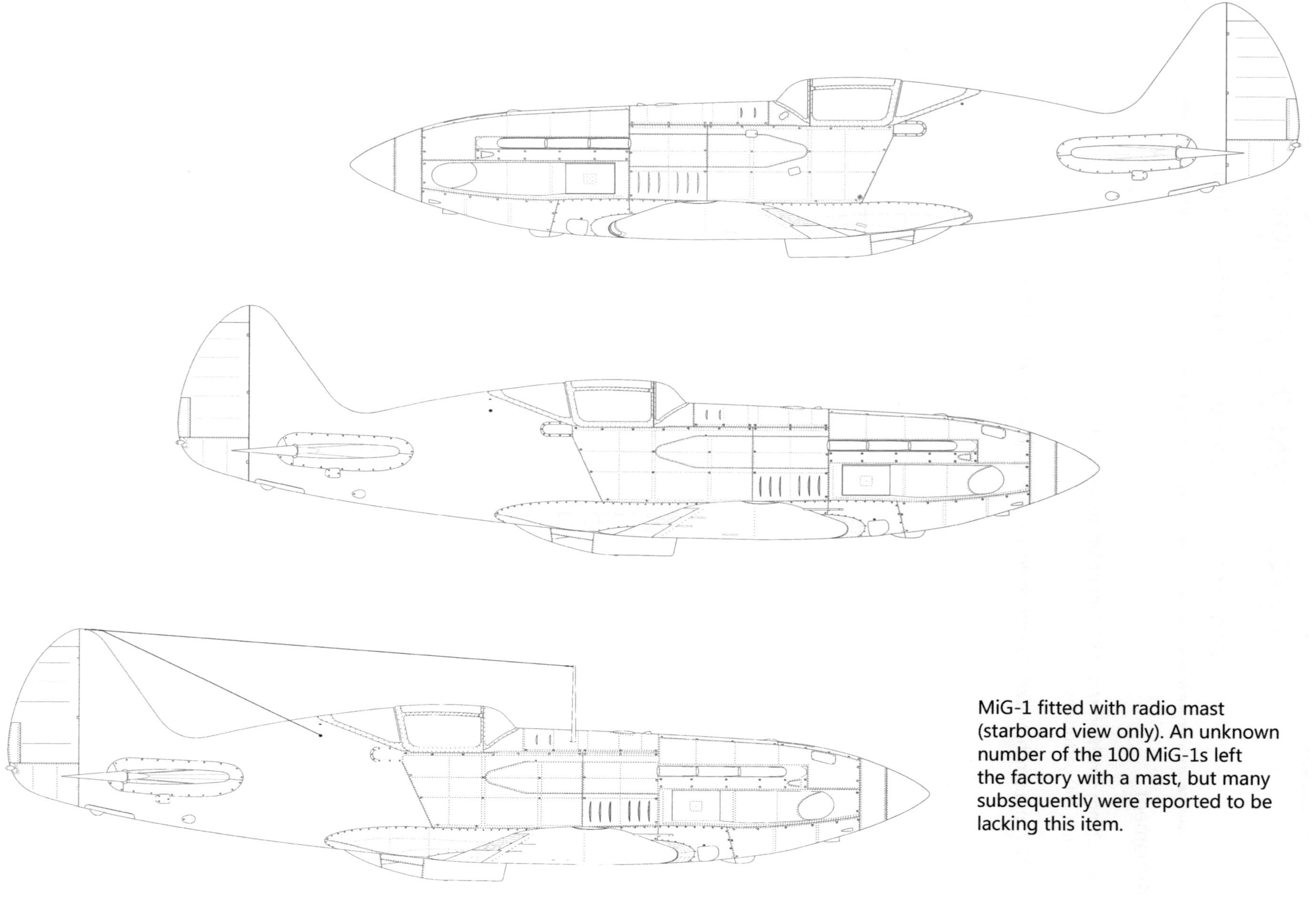

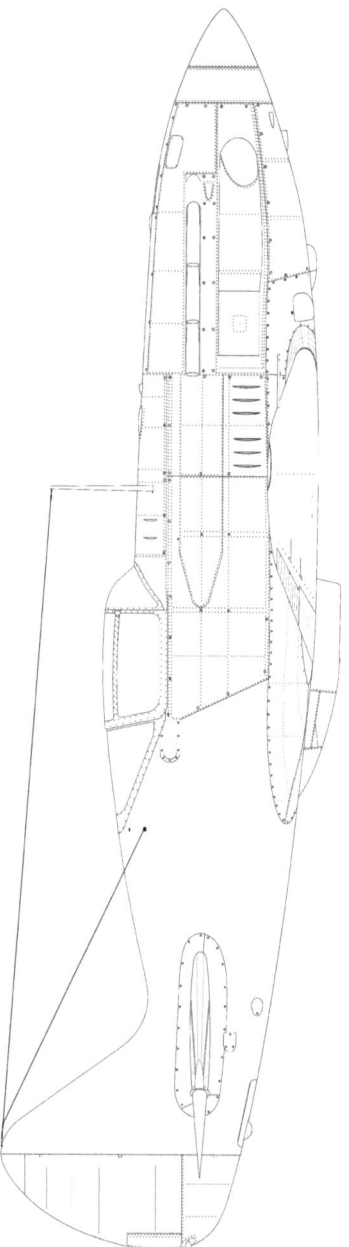

MiG-1 fitted with radio mast (starboard view only). An unknown number of the 100 MiG-1s left the factory with a mast, but many subsequently were reported to be lacking this item.

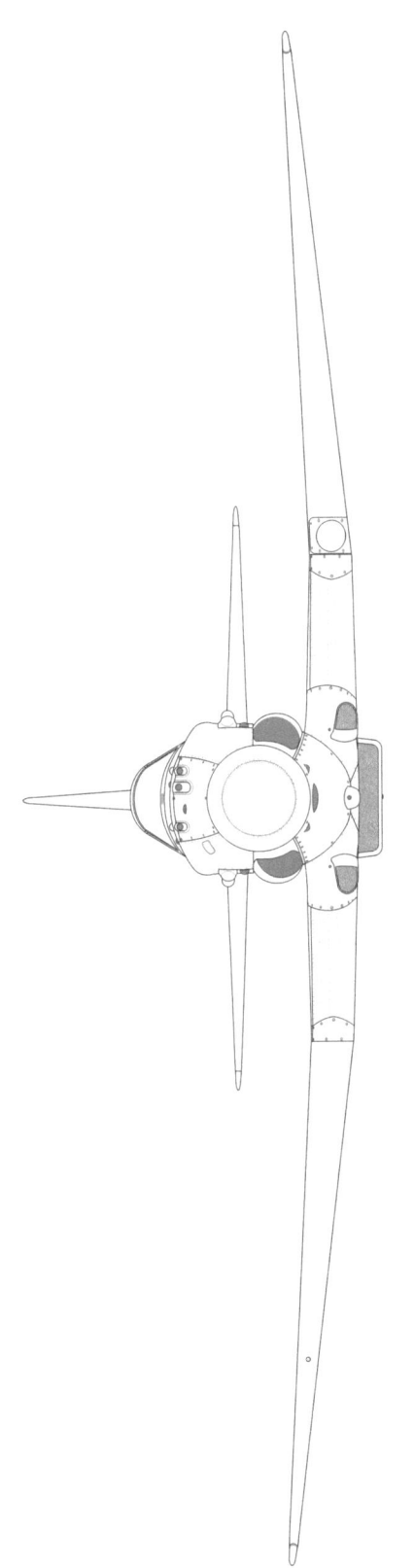

Note the 5° outer wing dihedral of the MiG-1

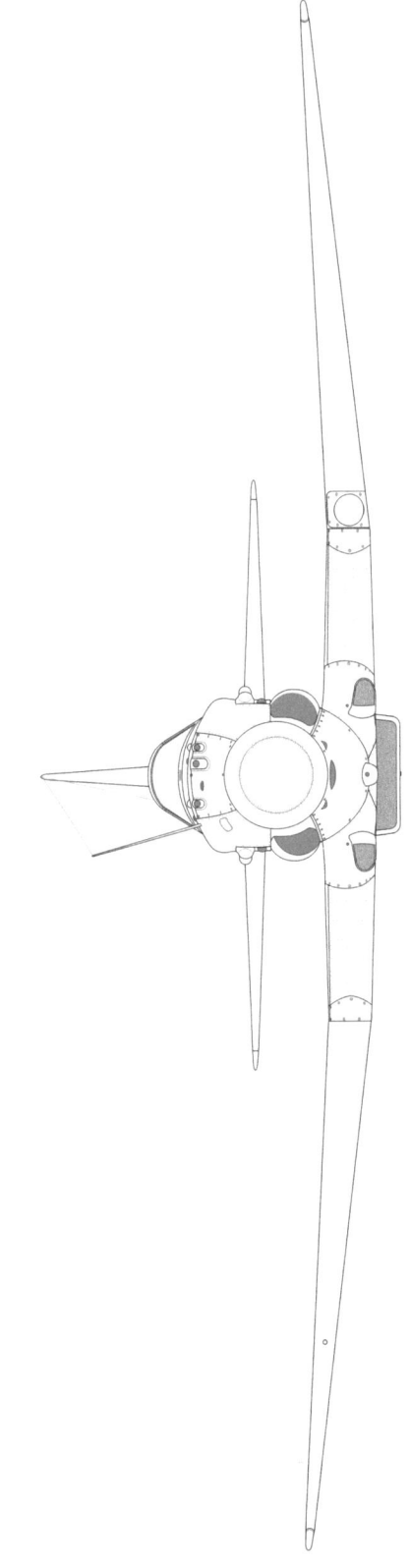

MiG-1 Front view showing radio mast

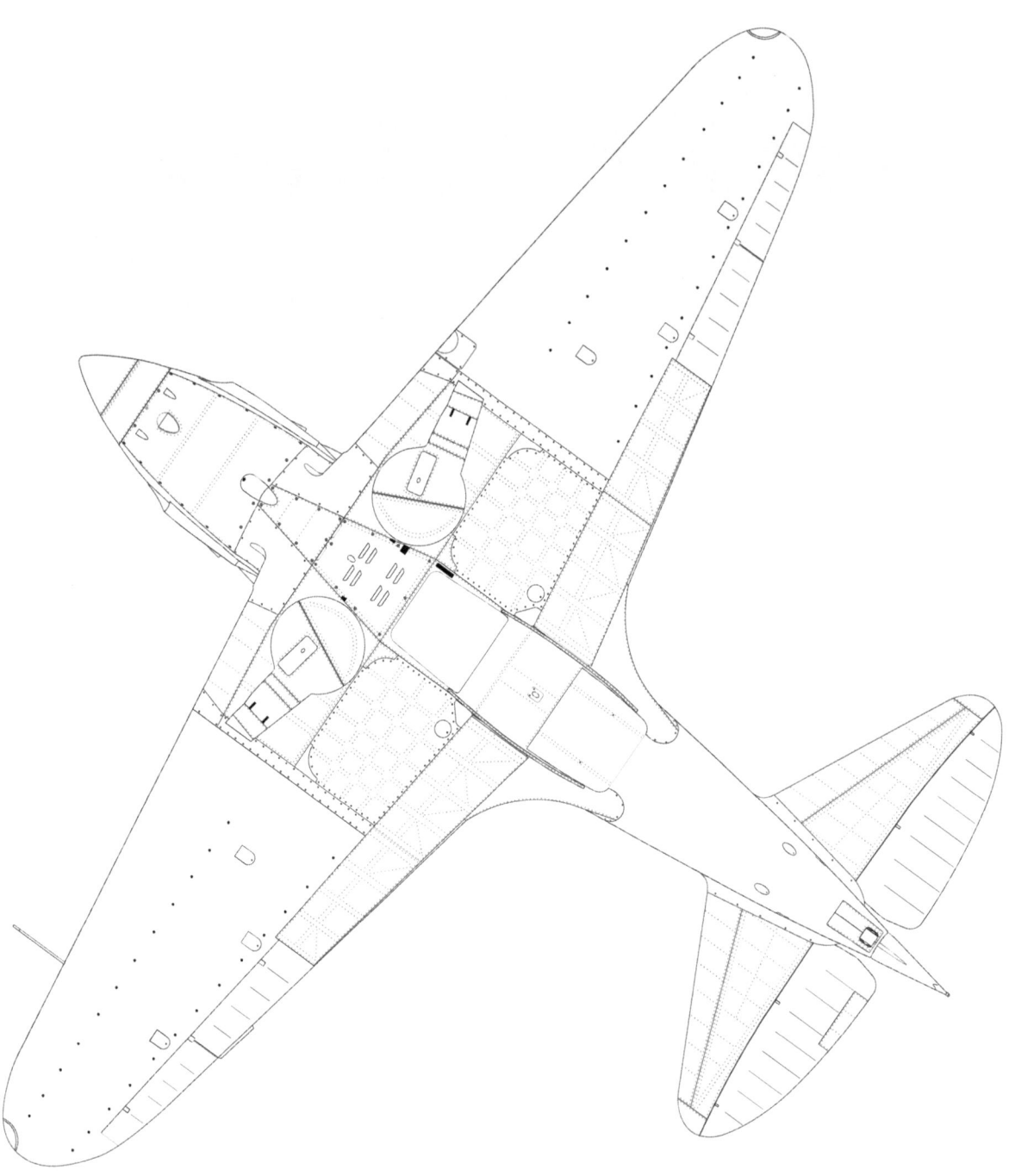

MiG-3 ca. P/N 2100-2300

(completed ~ December 1940 - January 1941)

Armament:

2 x 7.62 mm synchronised ShKAS mounted above engine
each with 750 cartridges

1 x 12.7 mm synchronised UBS mounted above engine with 300 cartridges

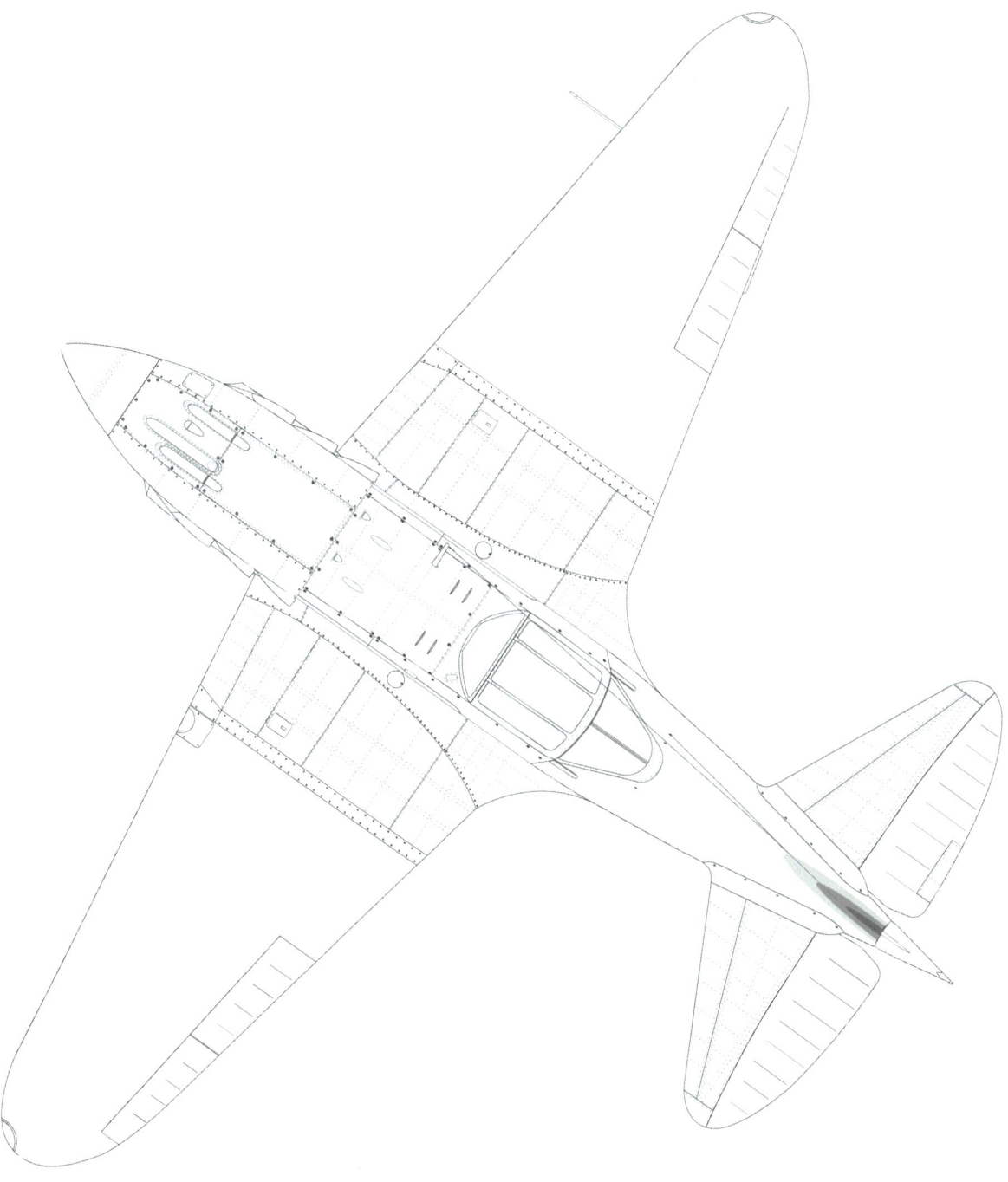

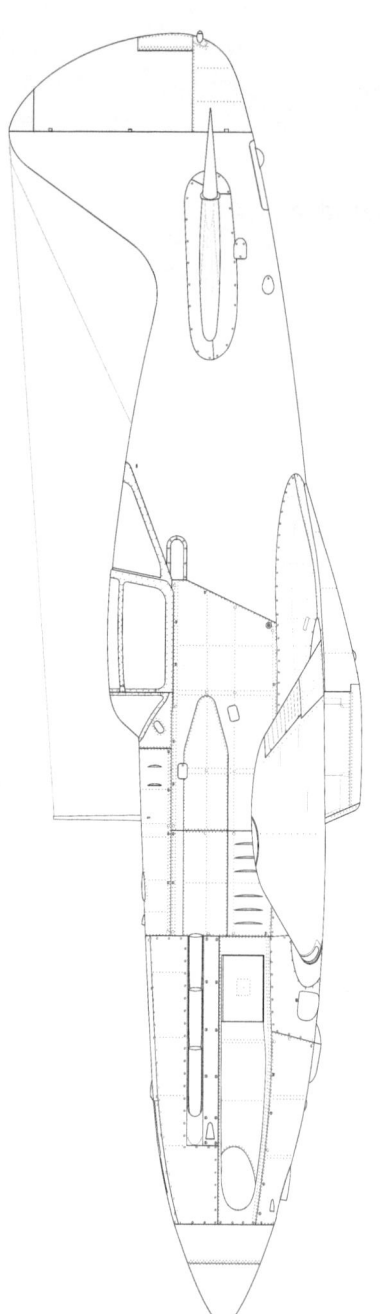
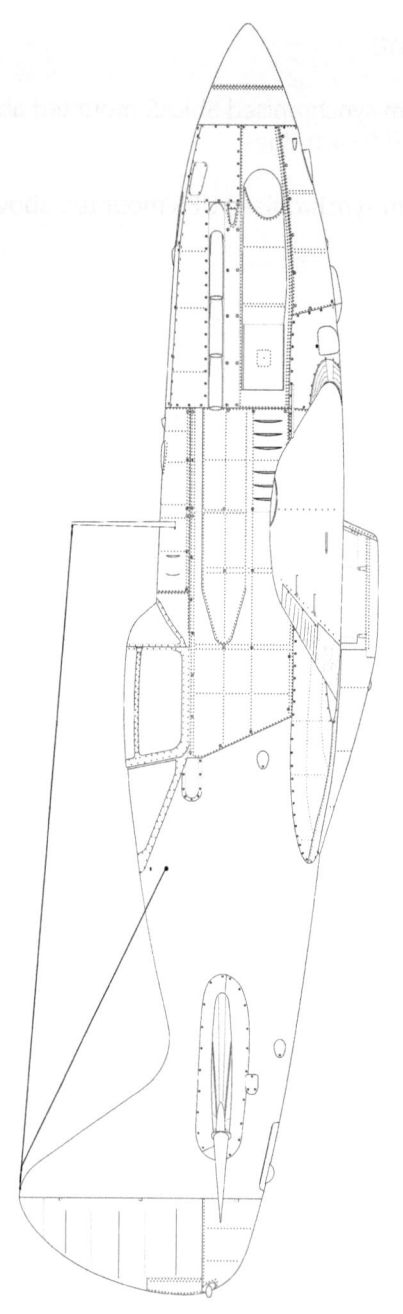

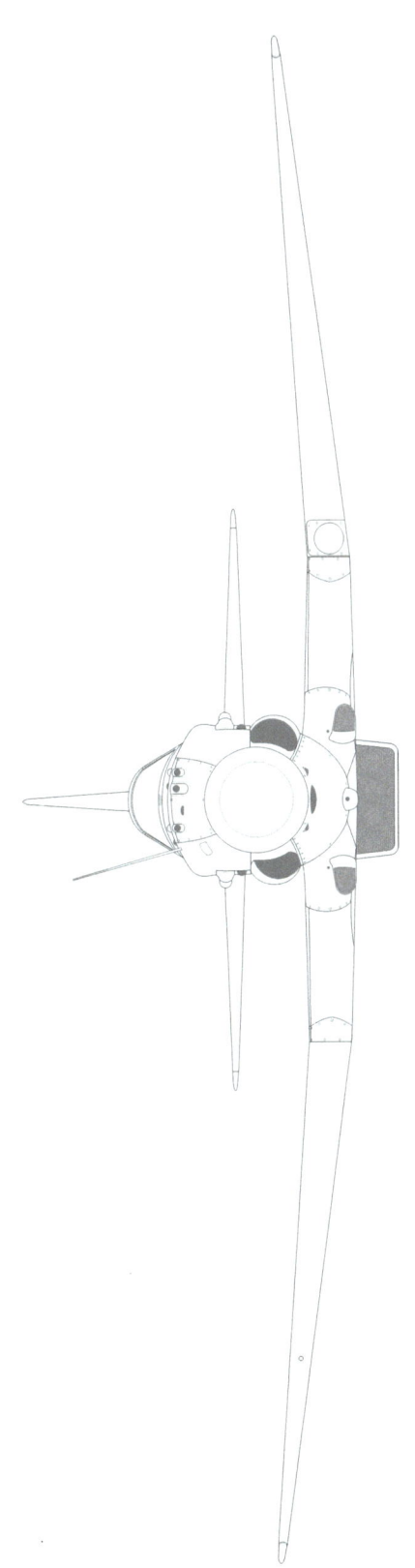

Main Feature Modifications:

• The early MiG-3s retained the short, aft mounted radio mast of the MiG-1

• They also retained the 'Yak' style surround type exhaust fairing

• With the lengthened nose, the entire lower central panel and access arrangement was completely modified

• No under wing fittings were seen on the p/n 2100-2300 aircraft

• The outer wing panel dihedral of all MiG-3s was increased to 6°

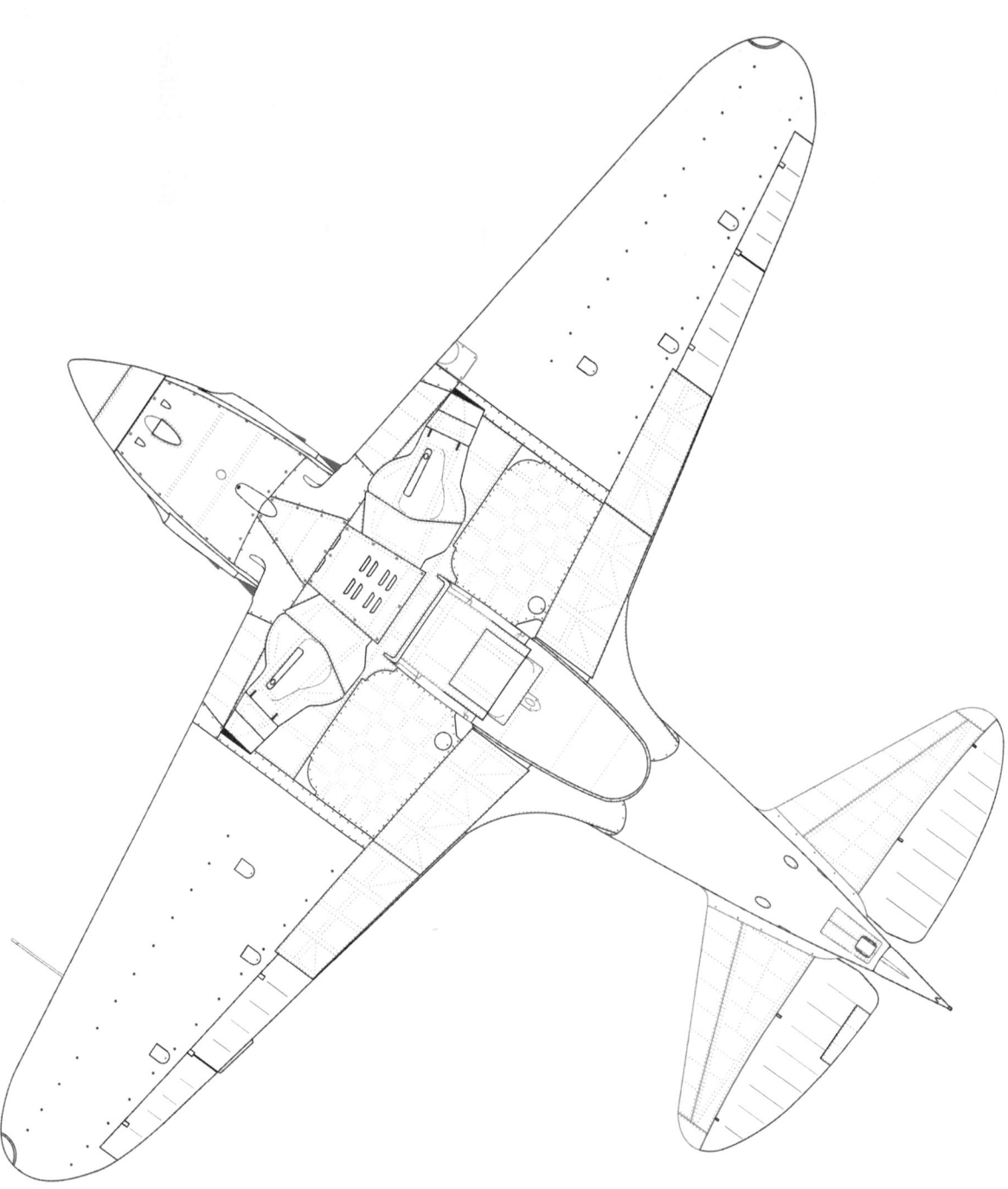

MiG-3 ca. P/N 2300-2650

(completed ~ February - March 1941)

Armament:

2 x 7.62 mm synchronised ShKAS mounted above engine
each with 750 cartridges

1 x 12.7 mm synchronised UBS mounted above engine with 300 cartridges

under-wing fittings to accommodate racks or various stores

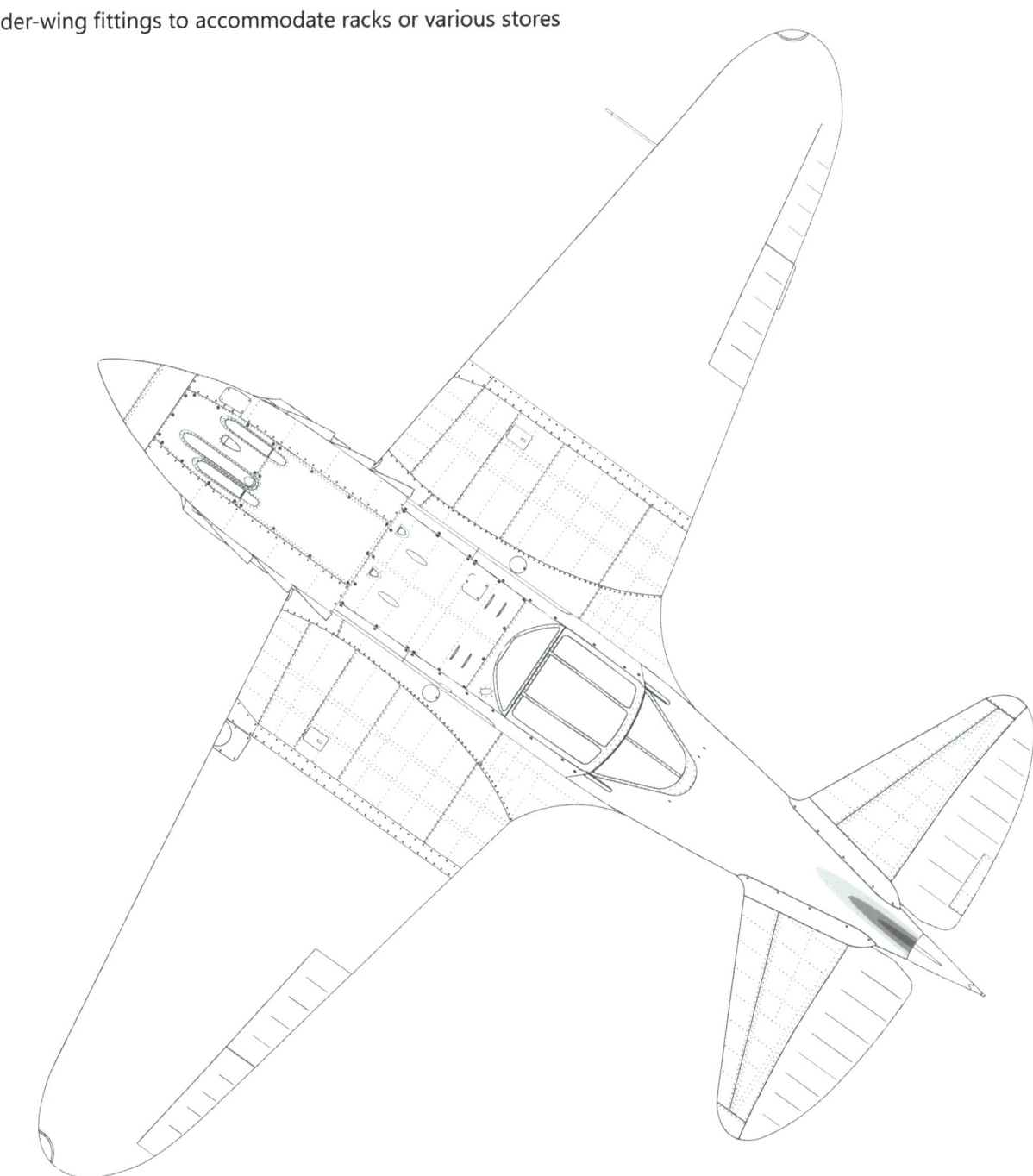

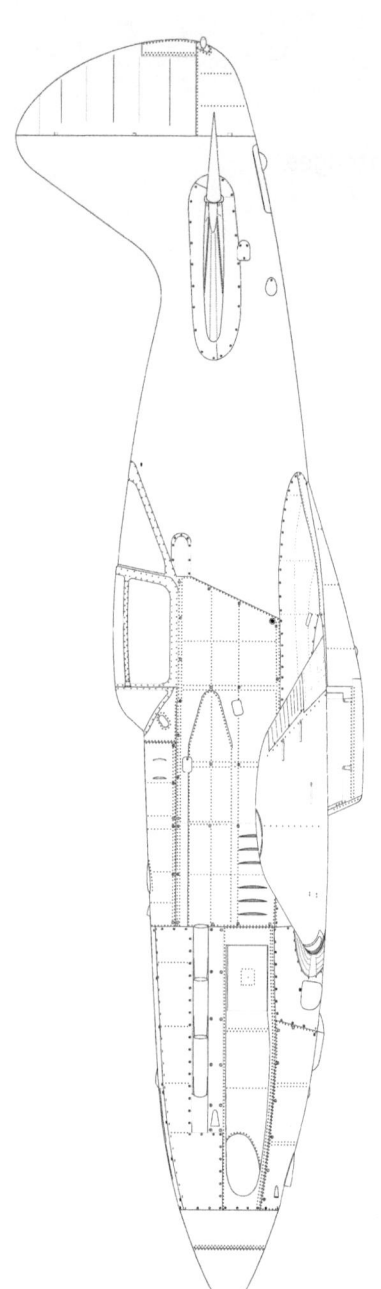

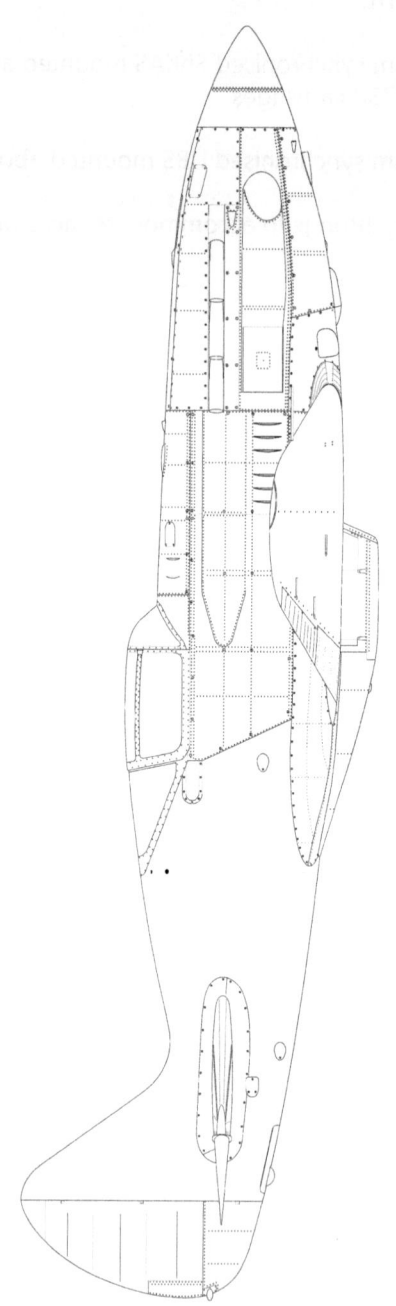

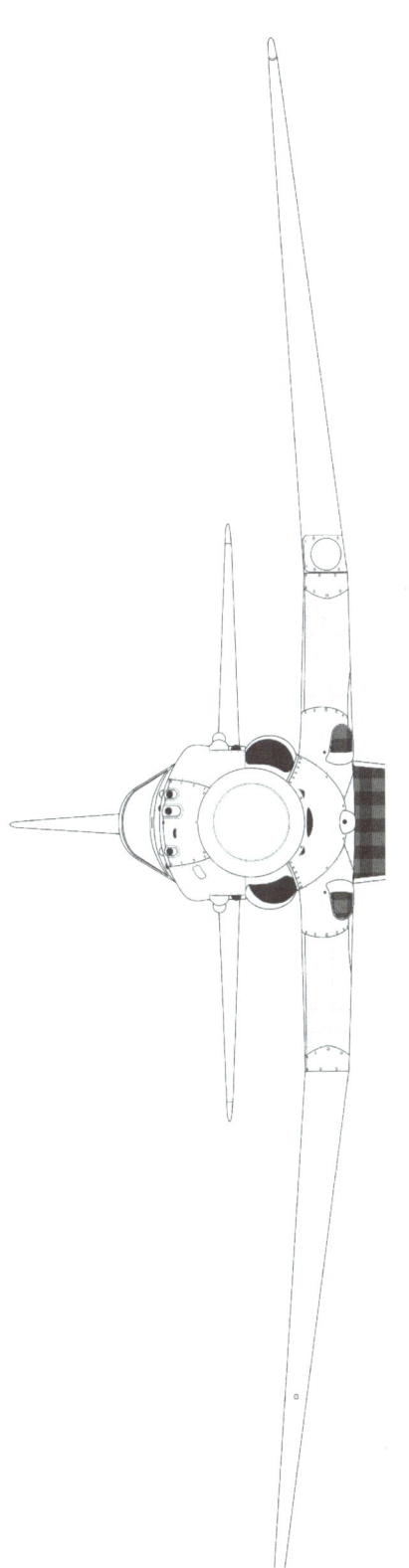

Main Feature Modifications:

- MiG-3s of the p/n 2300-2650 range were usually completed without a radio mast

- New exhaust arrangement with mini-fairing at the front

- Under wing threaded hole type fittings

- Filling and inspection hatch for fuselage fuel cell on upper port side ahead of windscreen

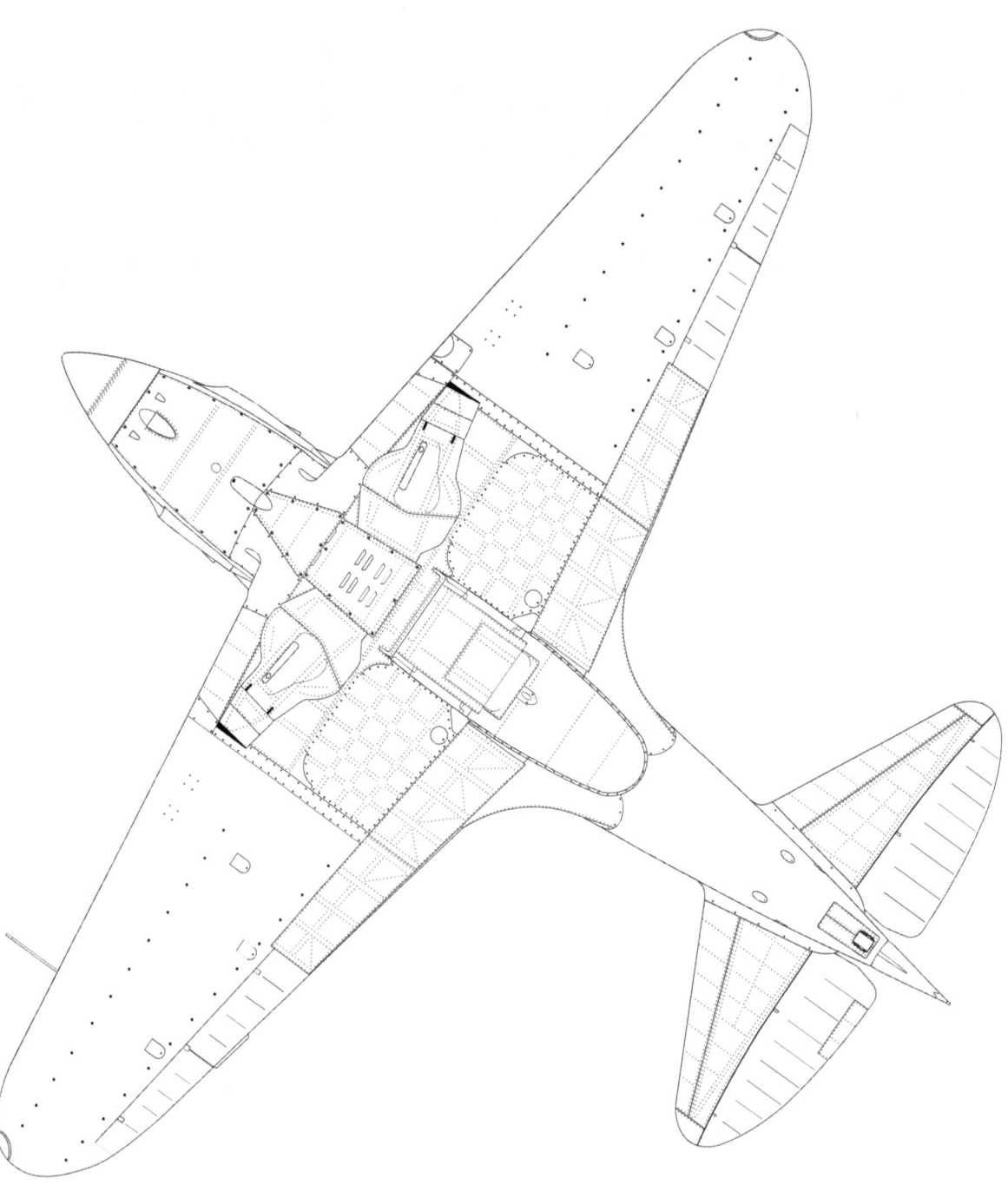

MiG-3 ca. P/N 2650-3400
(completed ~ April - *early* June 1941)

Armament:

2 x 7.62 mm synchronised ShKAS mounted above engine
each with 750 cartridges

1 x 12.7 mm synchronised UBS mounted above engine with 300 cartridges

2 x 12.7 mm BK in under-wing gunpods with 140 cartridges each

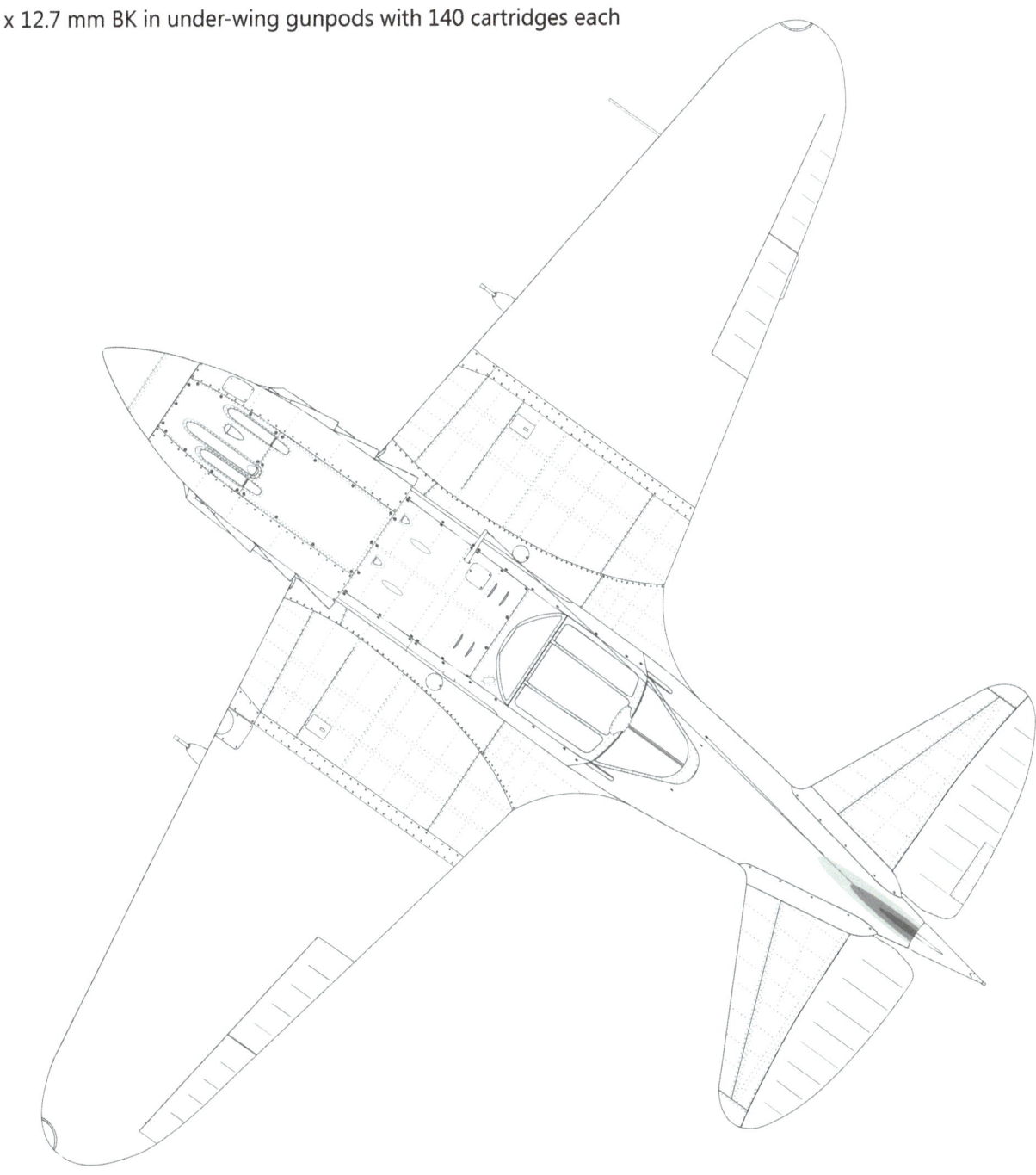

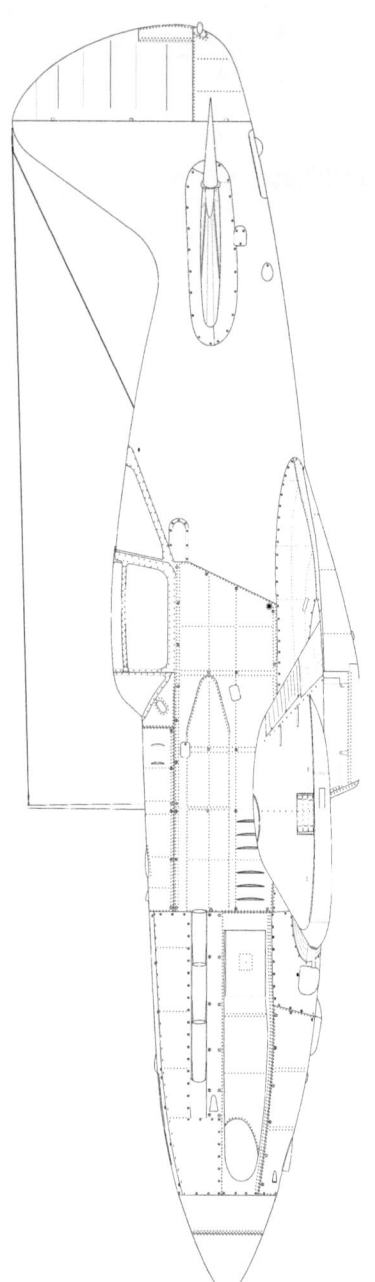

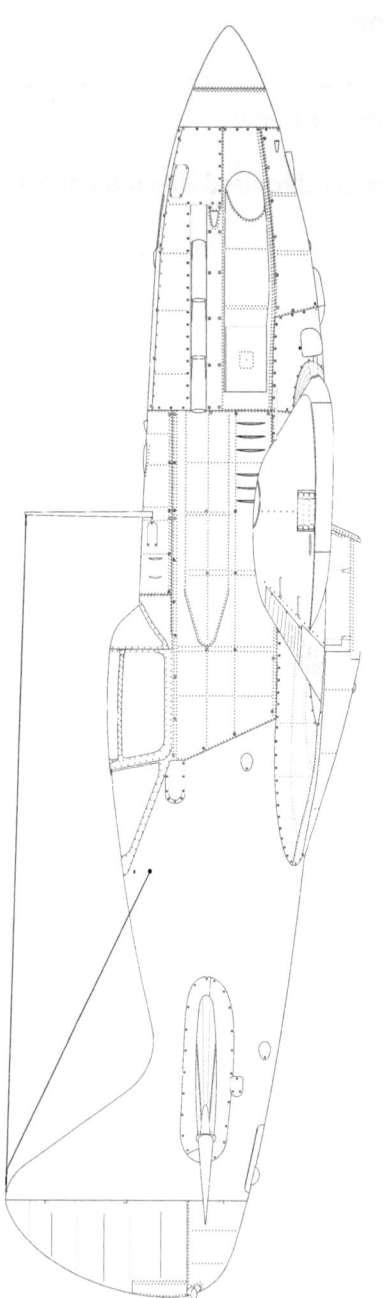

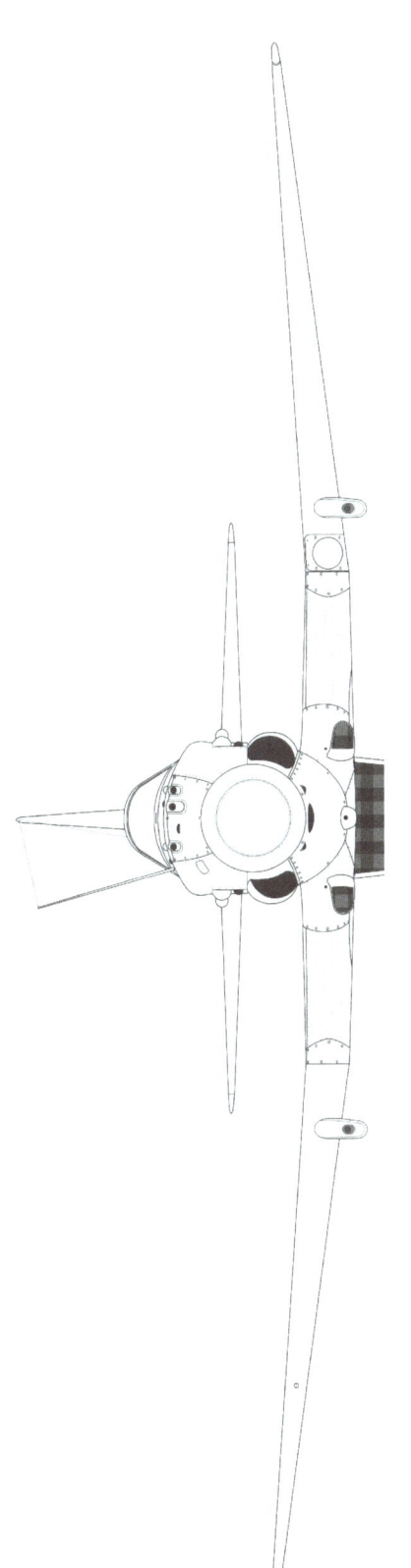

Main Feature Modifications:

• Typical (larger) radio mast w/aerials

• Under wing BK gun pods

• Under wing threaded hole type mounts for fittings

• Fillet on rear sliding canopy frame

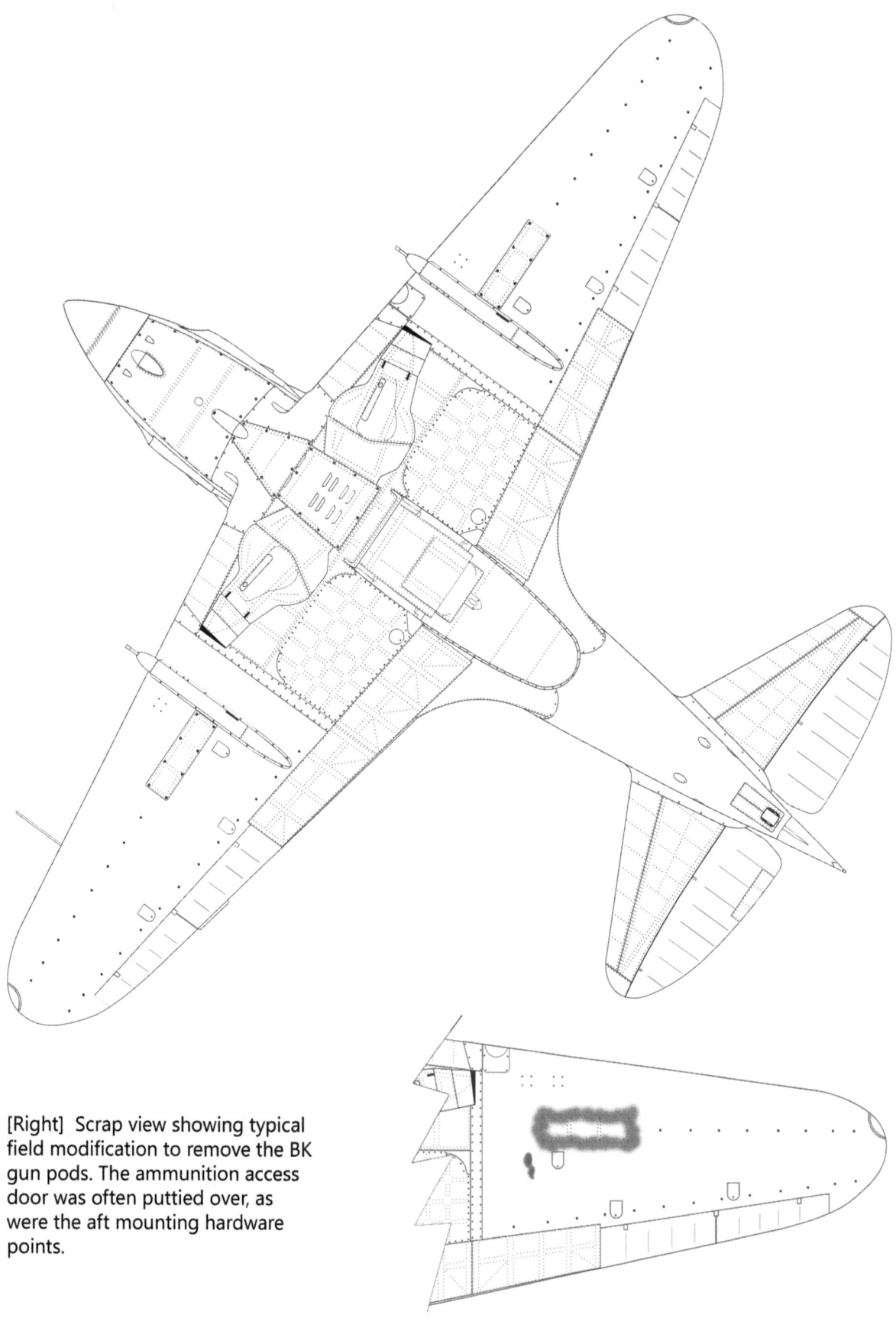

[Right] Scrap view showing typical field modification to remove the BK gun pods. The ammunition access door was often puttied over, as were the aft mounting hardware points.

MiG-3 ca. P/N 3400-3850

(completed ~ *mid* June - *mid* July 1941)

Armament:

2 x 7.62 mm synchronised ShKAS mounted above engine
each with 750 cartridges

1 x 12.7 mm synchronised UBS mounted above engine with 300 cartridges

under-wing fittings to accommodate six RS-82 rockets and associated rails,
gunpods or other stores

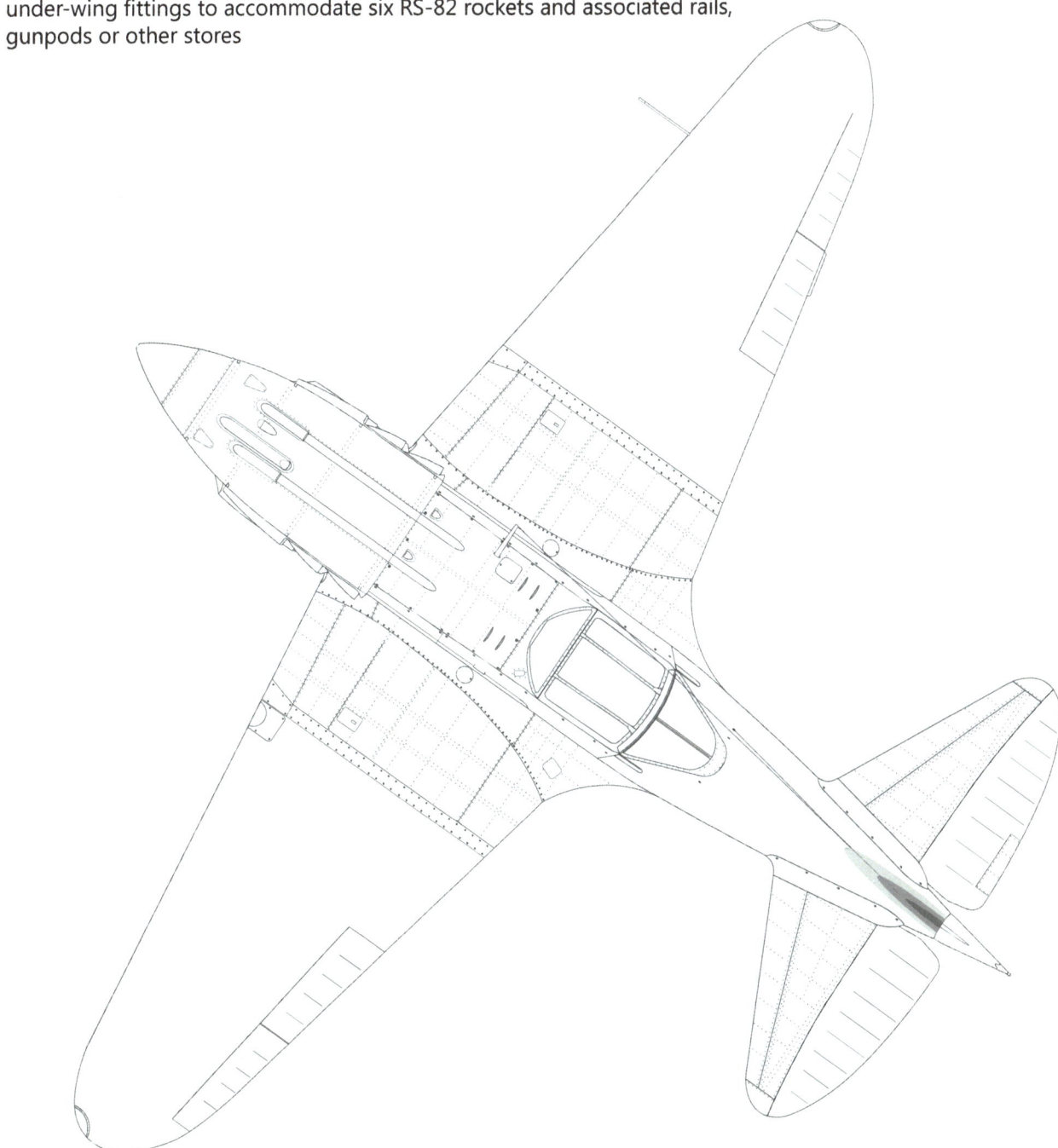

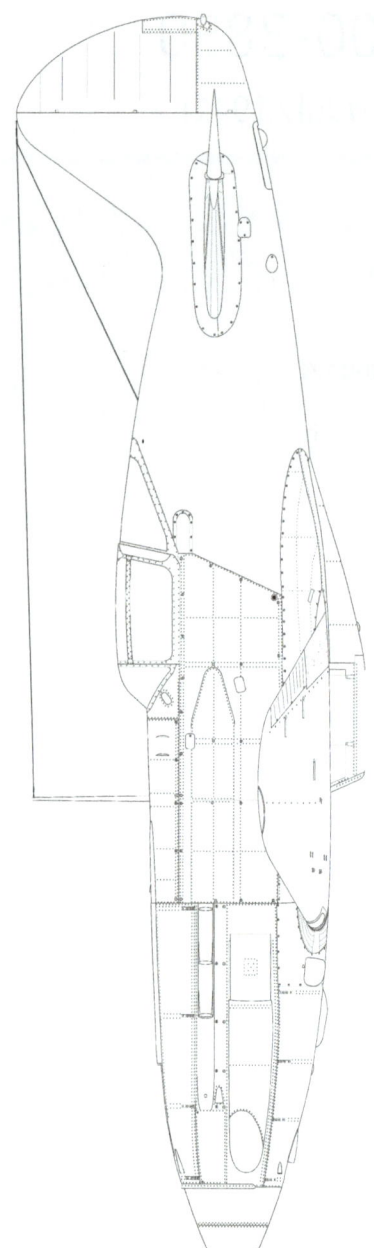

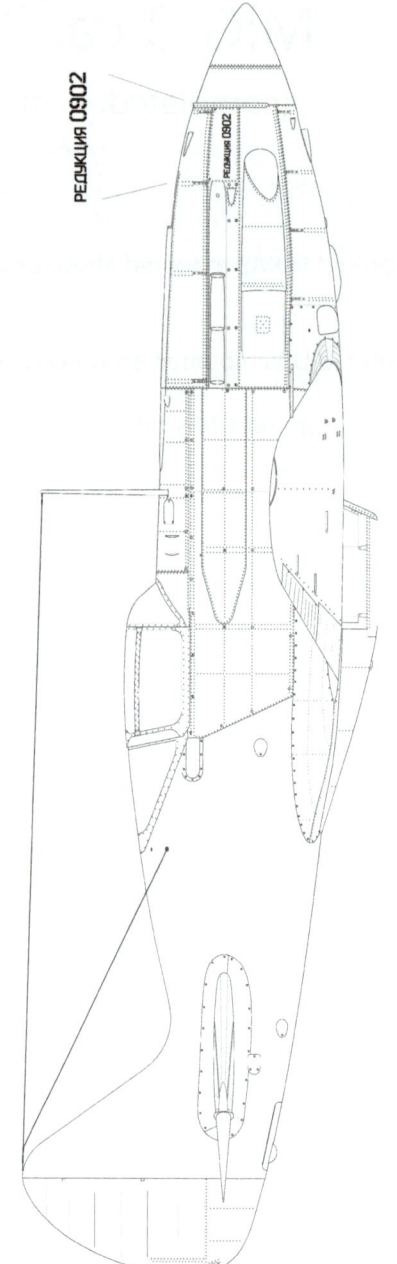

РЕДУКЦИЯ 0902

РЕДУКЦИЯ 0902

Aircraft in the range p/n 3400-3750, the first of the late style cowling types, were built with the original 0.902 gear reduction unit and VISh-22E propeller. When applied at the factory, the gear ratio stencil was normally seen only on the starboard side of the cowling.

Main Feature Modifications:

• New cowling type with latch fasteners [see page 65]

• New sliding canopy with glass rear section

• 'Universal' under wing fittings with 'eyelet' bolt mountings, round electrical access covers and threaded holes

• New blister type fairings over the guns

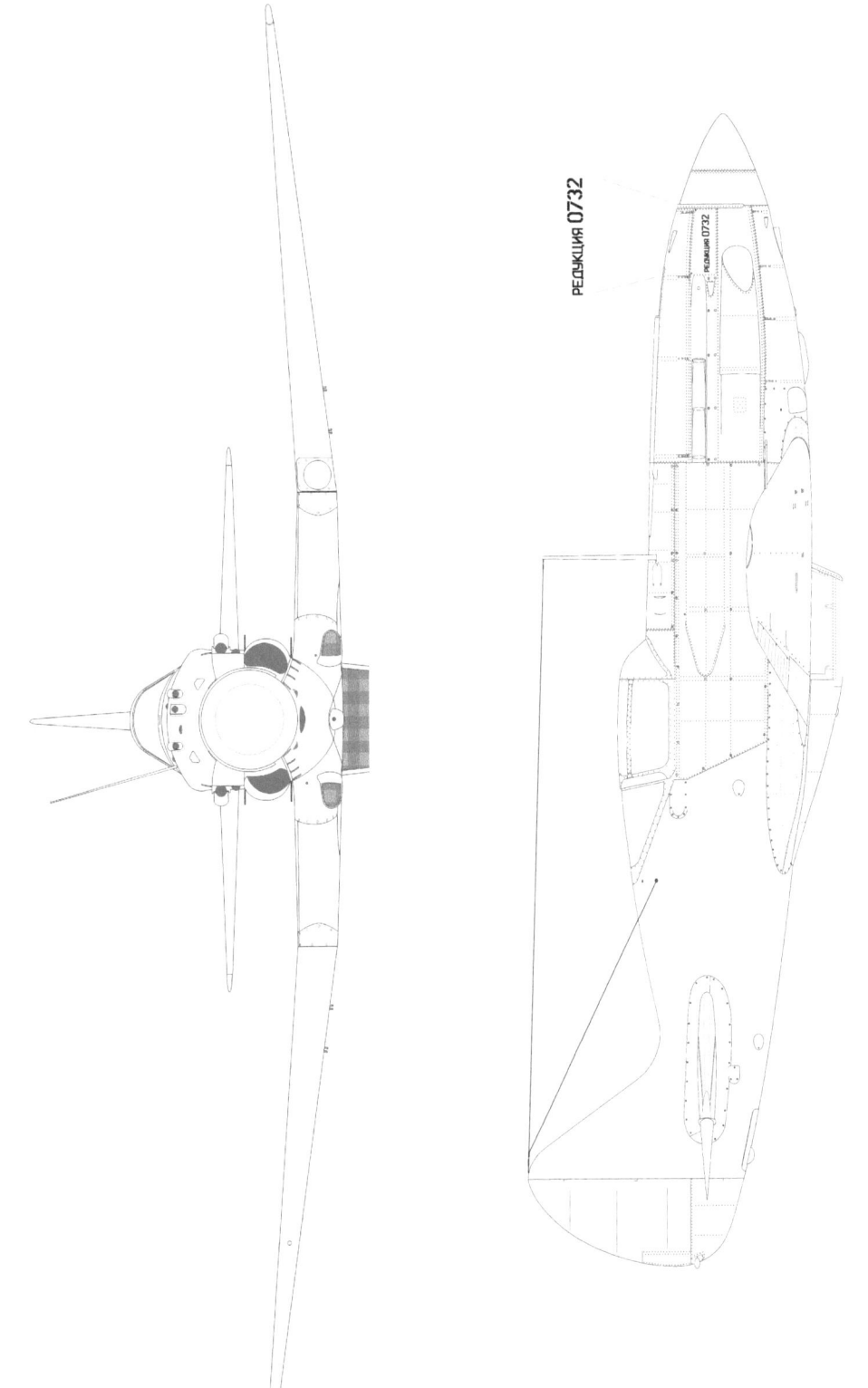

РЕДУКЦИЯ 0732

The final 100, or so, aircraft of this group (approximately p/n 3750-3850) were completed with the new 0.732 gear reduction unit and VISh-22K constant speed propeller. When applied at the factory, the gear ratio stencil was normally seen only on the starboard side of the cowling.

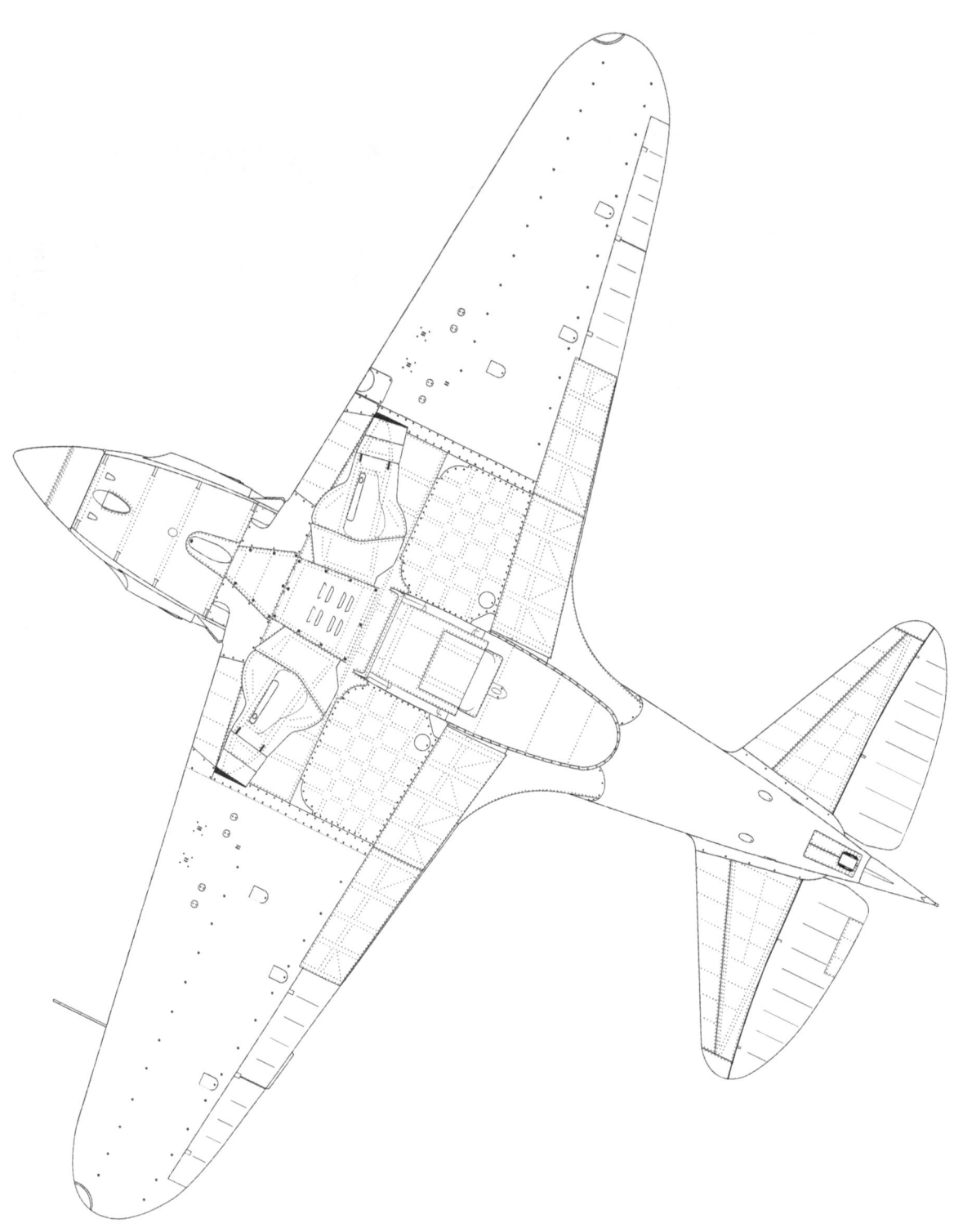

MiG-3 ca. P/N 3850-4400

(completed ~ *mid* July - *mid* August 1941)

Armament:

2 x 7.62 mm synchronised ShKAS mounted above engine
each with 750 cartridges

1 x 12.7 mm synchronised UBS mounted above engine with 300 cartridges

under-wing fittings to accommodate six RS-82 rockets and associated rails,
gunpods or other stores

[Left] Starboard side view with rocket rails mounted under wings

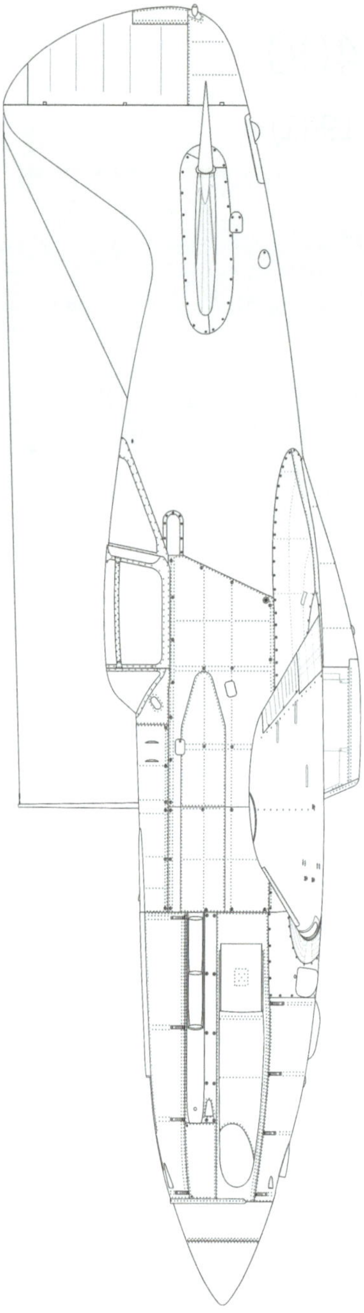

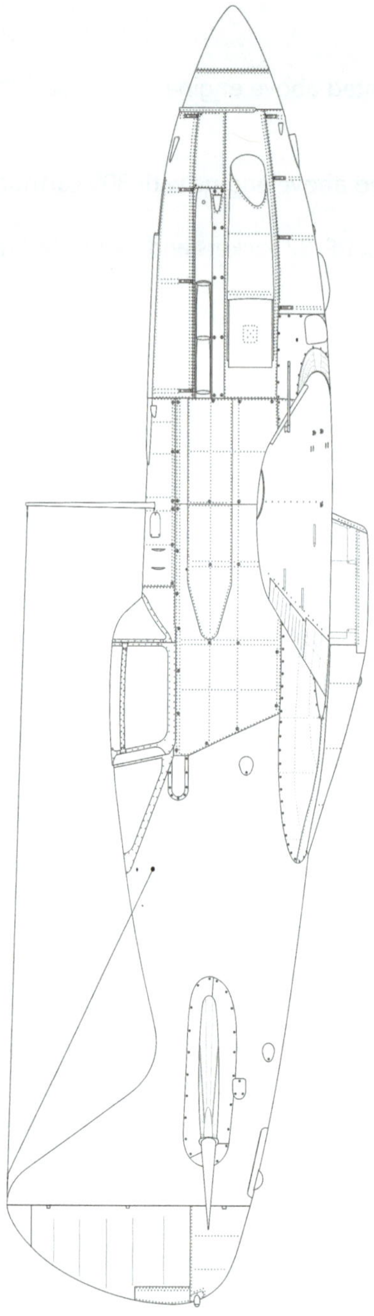

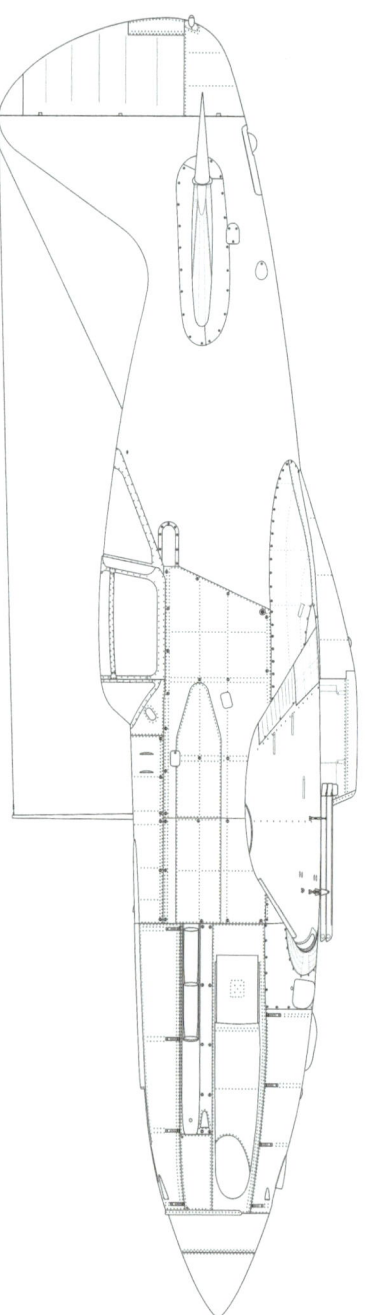

Main Feature Modifications:

- Leading edge wing slats with new pitot

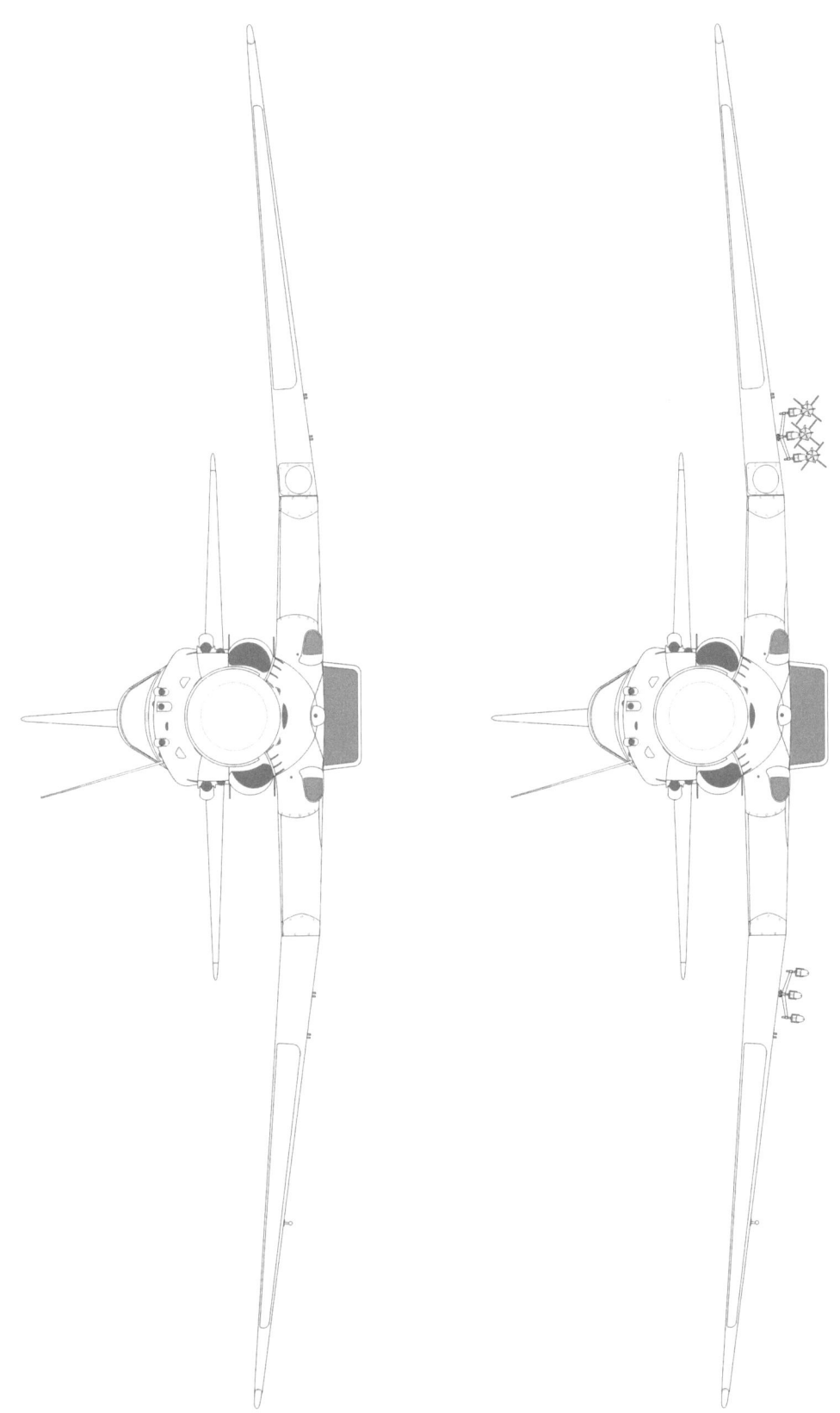

Front view showing rocket rails fitted (to starboard), and rocket rails with RS-82 missiles (to port)

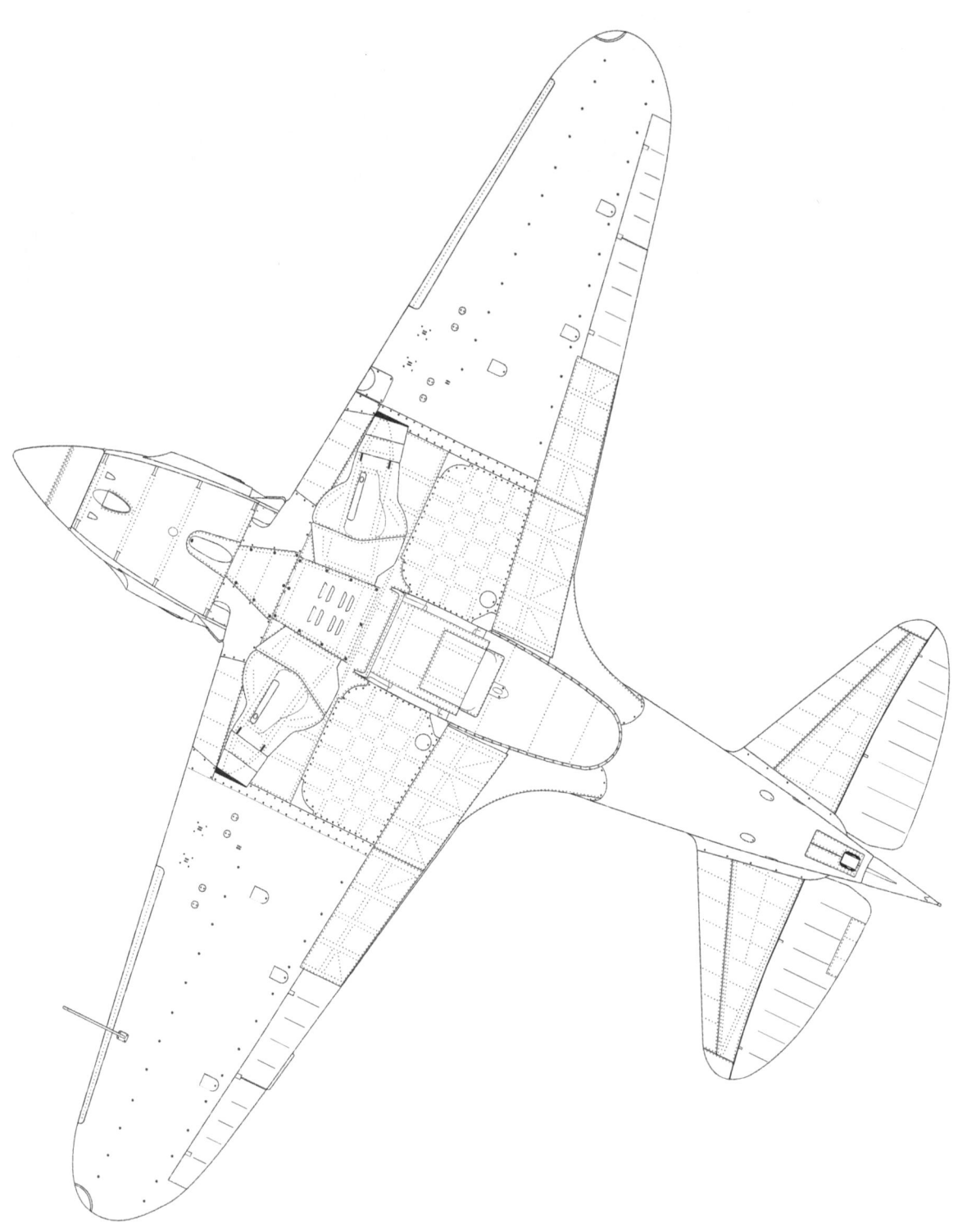

A fair number of MiG-3s in the p/n 3850-4400 block were delivered from Factory 1 with six rocket rails installed. The starboard wing shows only the rails fitted, whilst the port wing features the RS-82 rockets mounted on rails, for comparison.

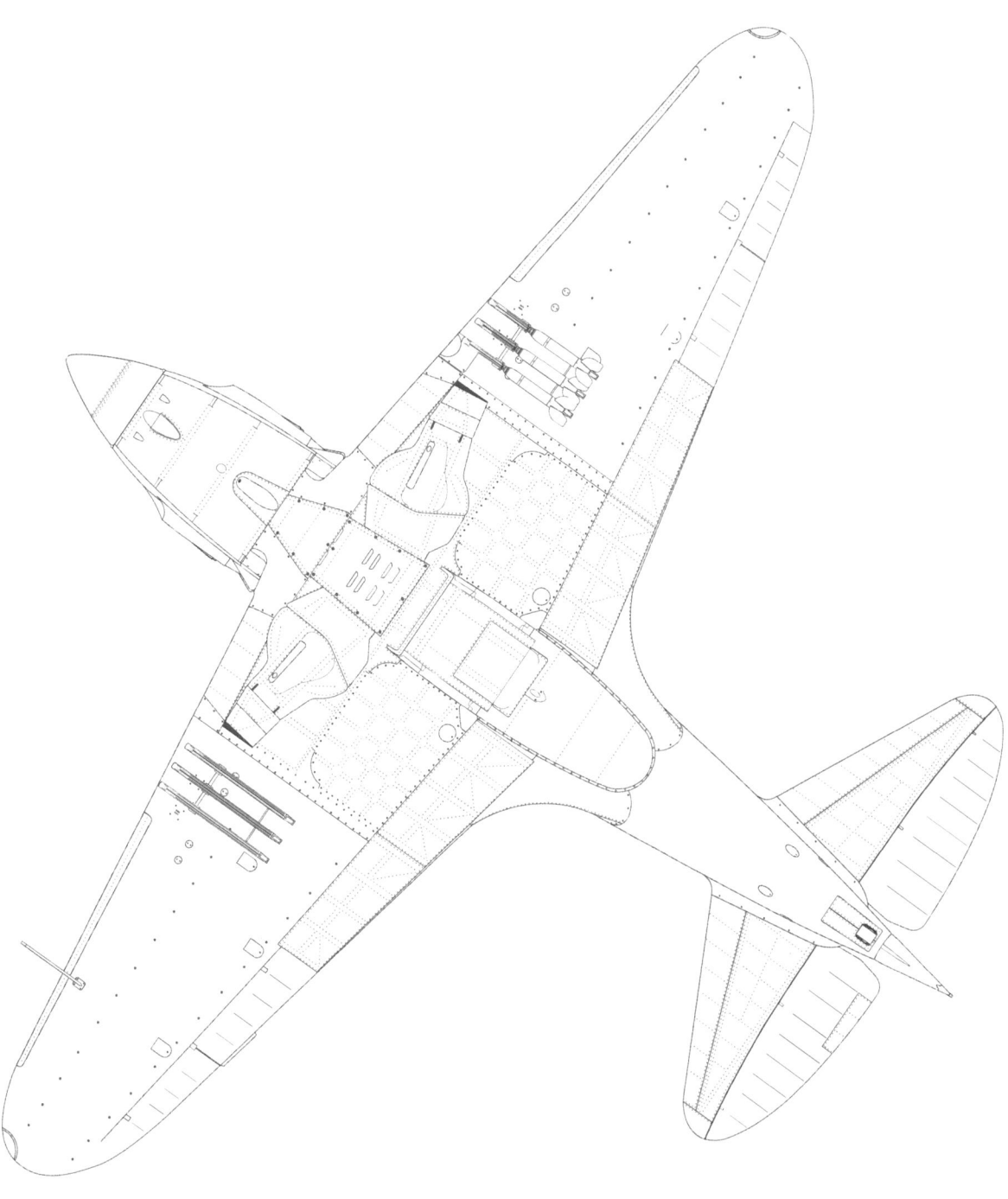

MiG-3 ca. P/N 4400-4950

(completed ~ *mid* August - *mid* September 1941)

Armament:

2 x 7.62 mm synchronised ShKAS mounted above engine
each with 750 cartridges

1 x 12.7 mm synchronised UBS mounted above engine with 300 cartridges

under-wing fittings to accommodate six RS-82
rockets and associated rails, gunpods or other stores

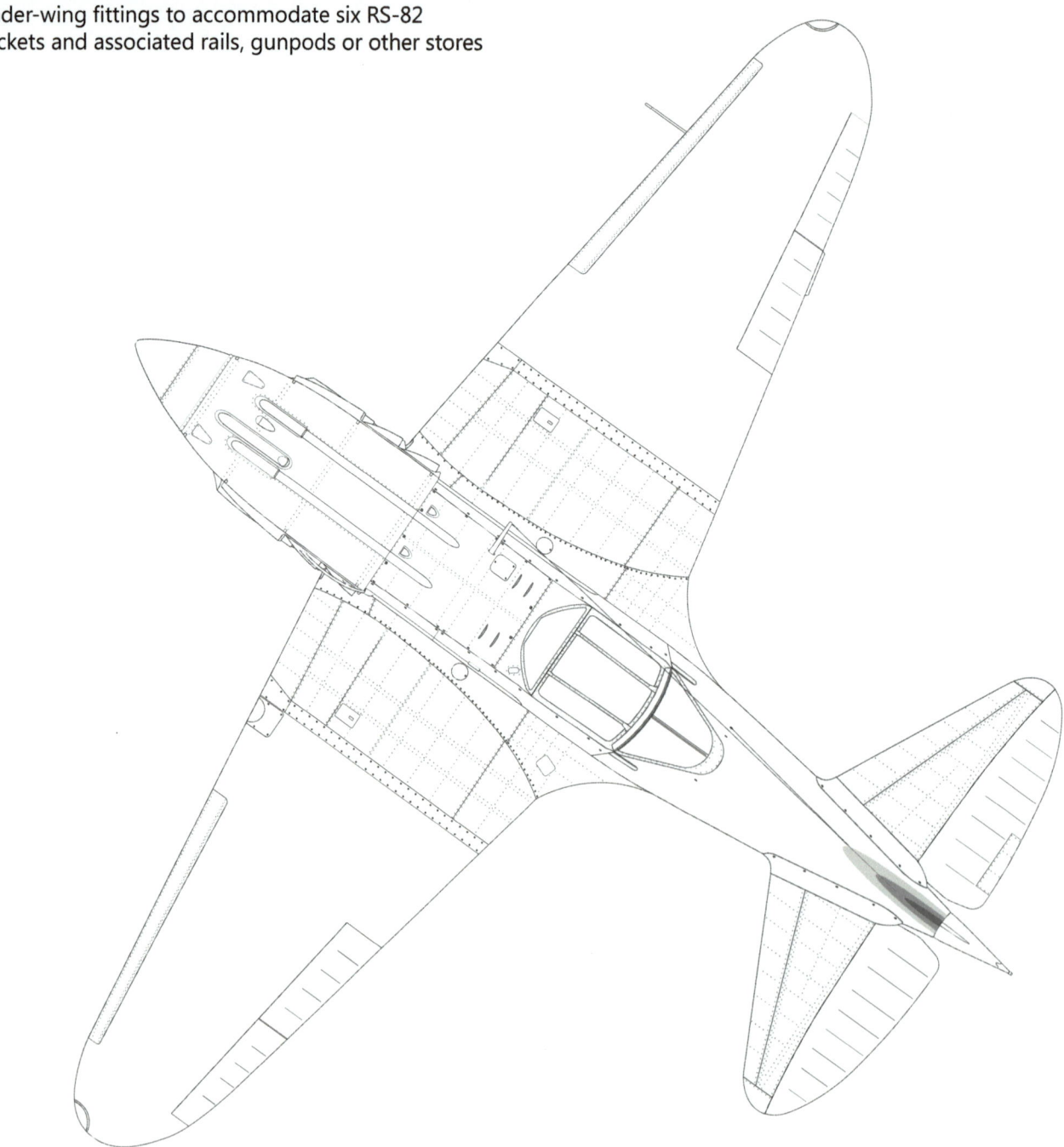

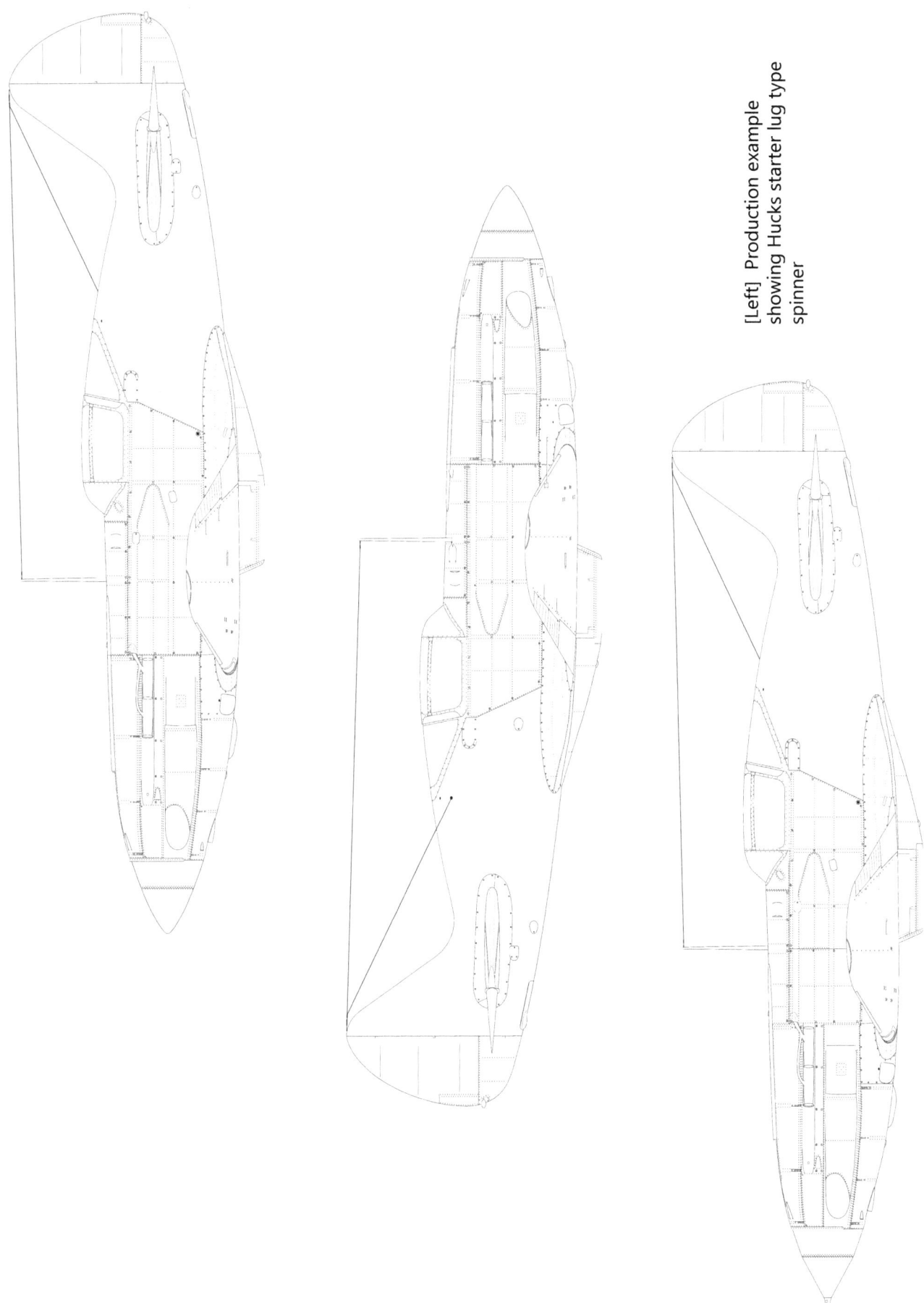

[Left] Production example
showing Hucks starter lug type
spinner

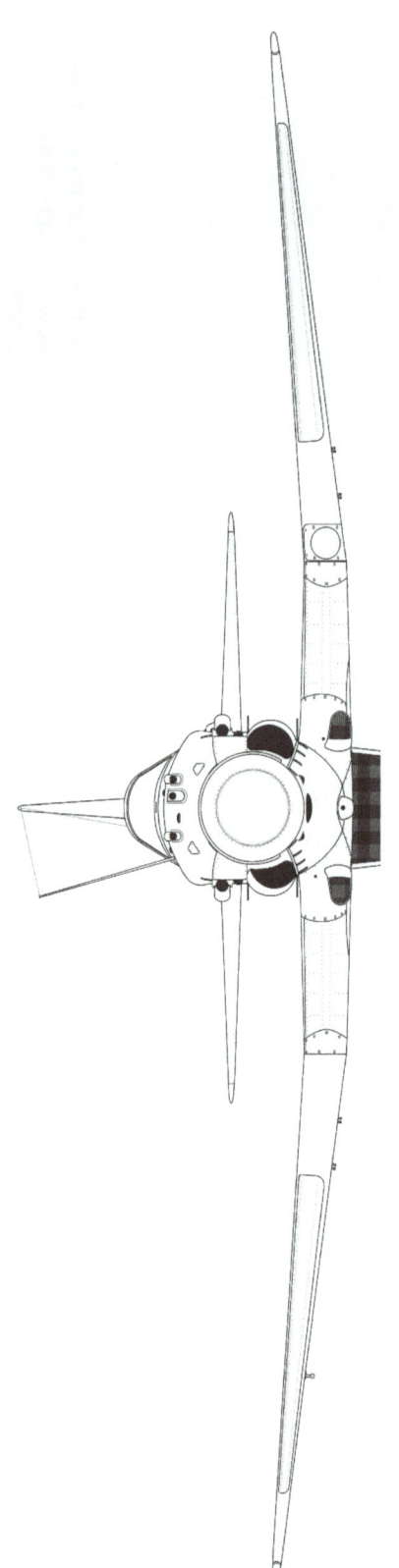

Main Feature Modifications:

- 'Clam shell' type enclosed tail wheel doors

- Inert gas collection tube on port side exhaust stacks

- An unknown number of these models were built with a modified spinner accommodating a Hucks starter collar

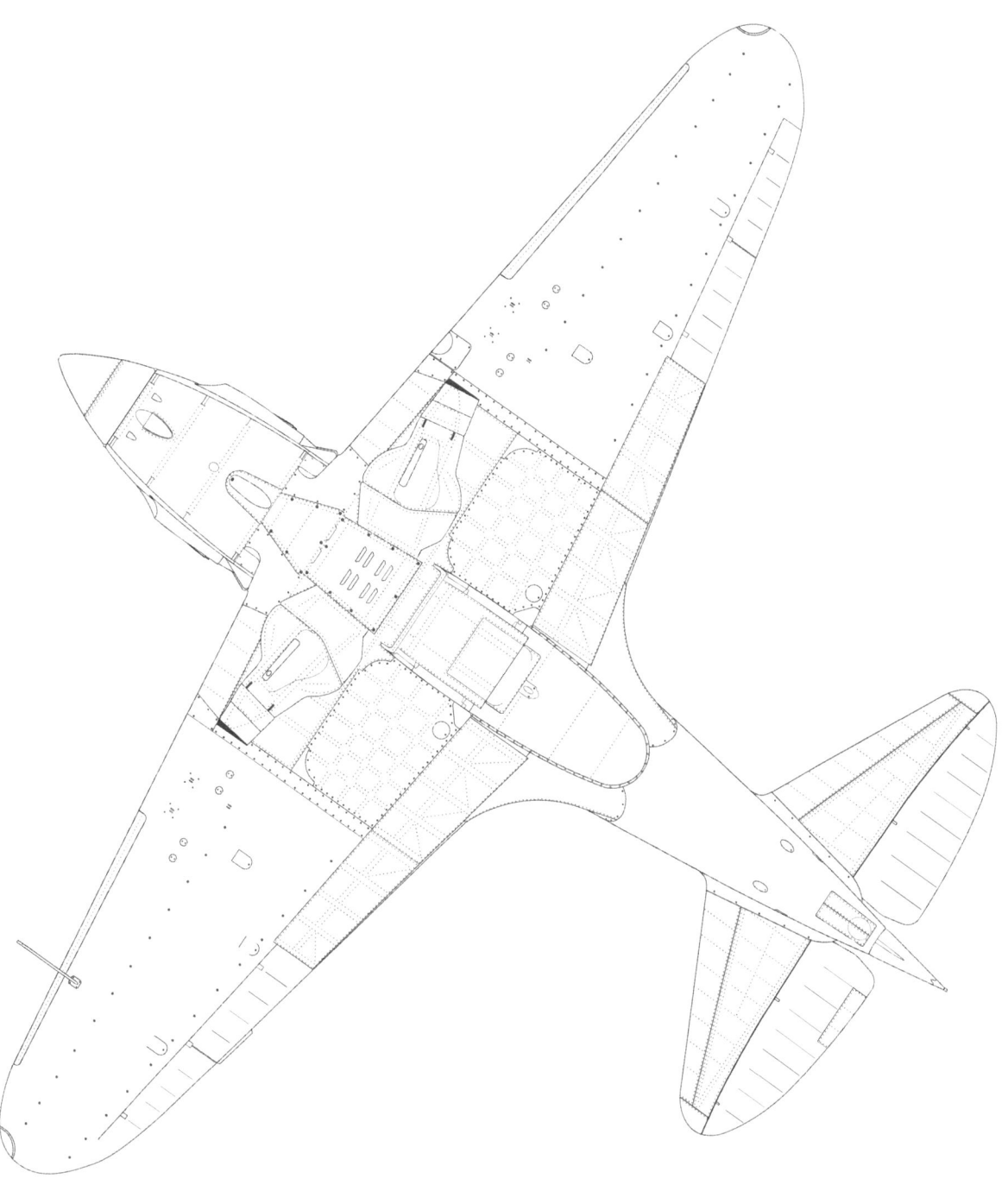

MiG-3 ca. P/N 4950-5250

(completed ~ *mid* September - *early* October 1941)

Armament:

2 x 12.7 mm synchronised UBS mounted above engine each with 360 cartridges

under-wing fittings to accommodate six RS-82 rockets and associated rails, gunpods or other stores

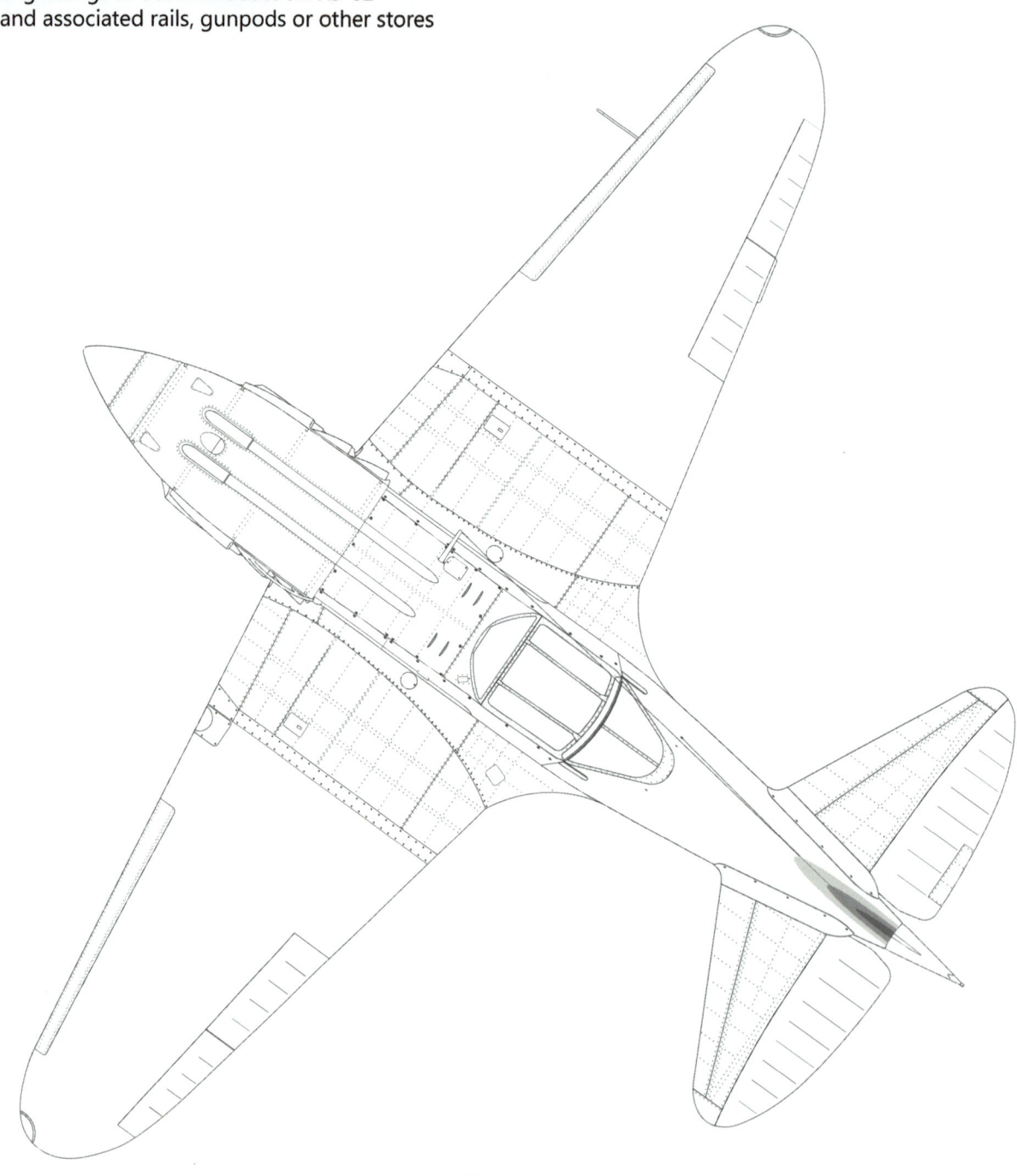

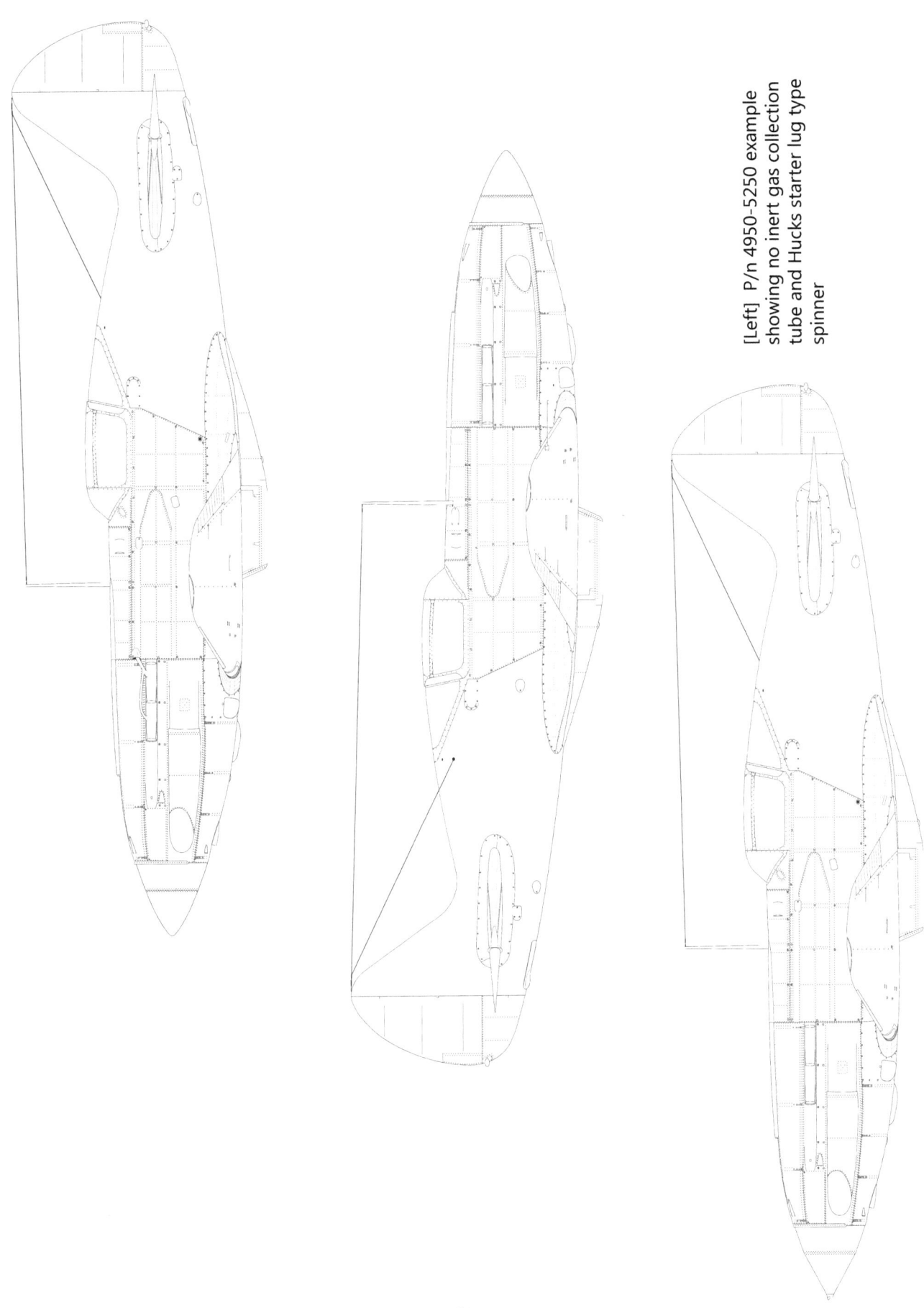

[Left] P/n 4950-5250 example showing no inert gas collection tube and Hucks starter lug type spinner

61

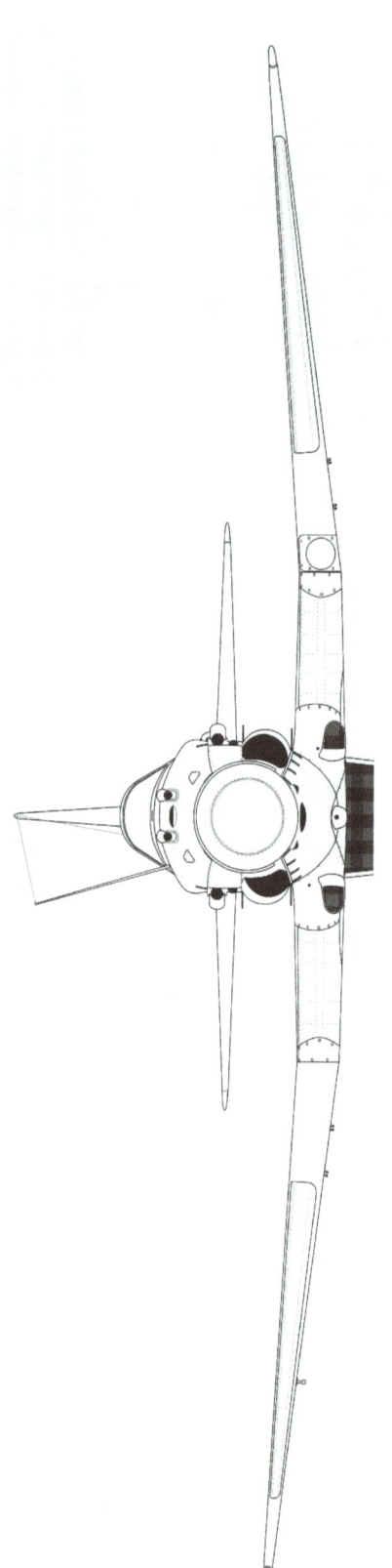

Main Feature Modifications:

- Revised upper cowling with larger gun fairings
- Small intake scoops on upper cowling removed
- Models built with and without inert gas tube and Hucks starter type spinner
- Larger central scoop on nose

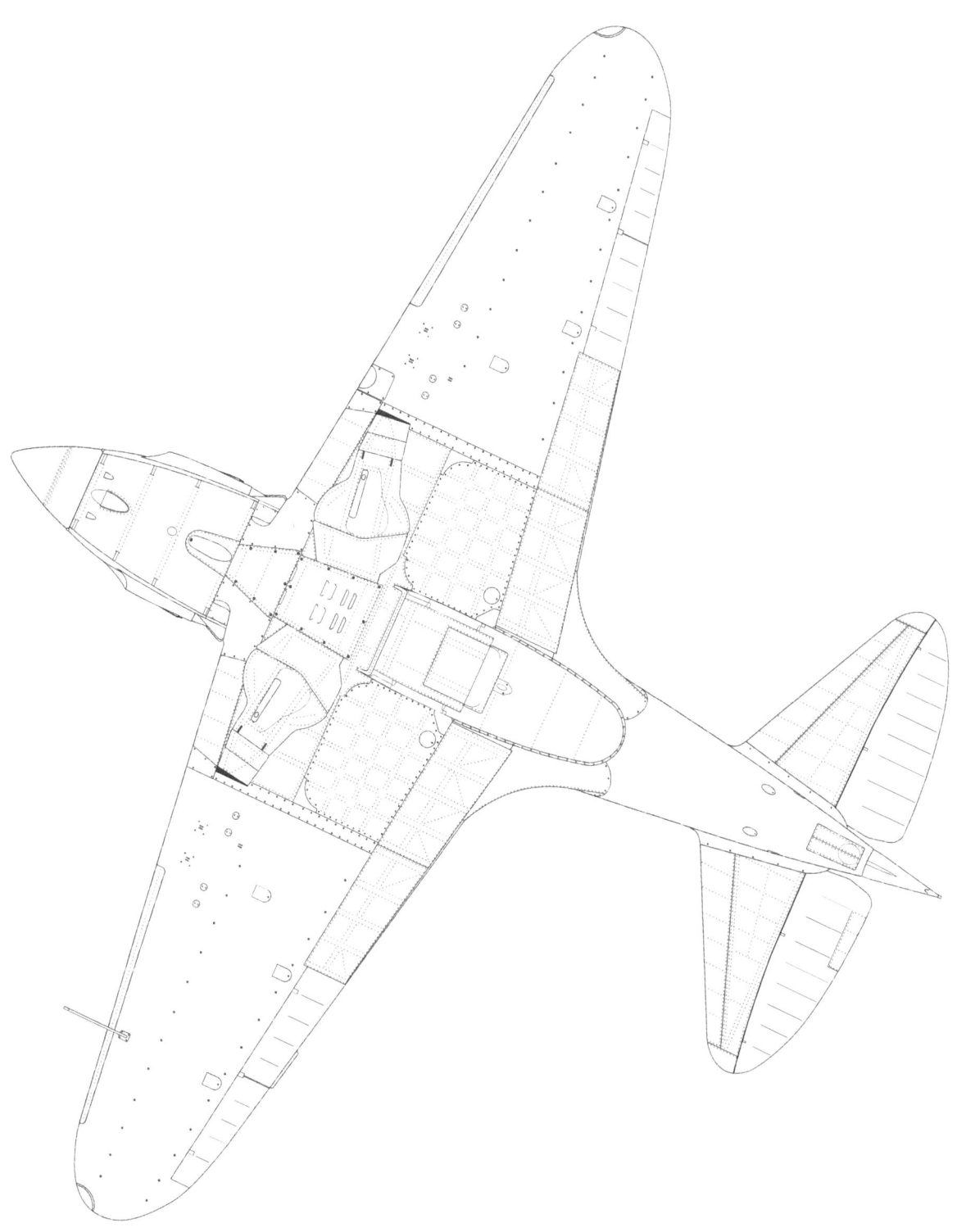

MiG-3 ca. P/N 6001-6030

(completed ~ April 1942)

Armament:

2 x 20 mm synchronised ShVAK mounted above engine each with 140 cartridges

unknown if under-wing fittings applied to this model

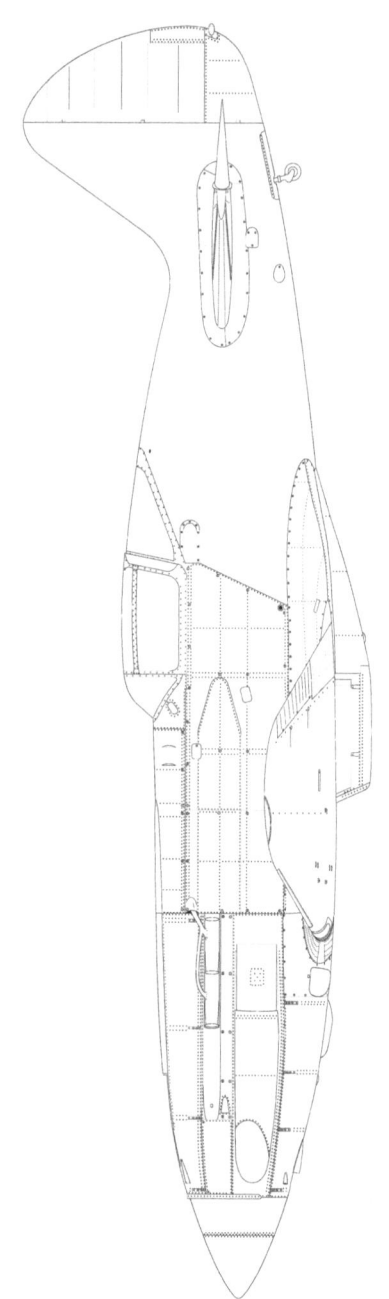

Once Factory No.1 had relocated to Kuibishev, the various MiG-3 components which had been evacuated with the rest of the production material were assembled into completed aircraft. Little is known about these machines, in fact, but they were, ironically, given the best armament package of any MiG fighter by pure chance. The main product at the new facility was to be the Il-2, for whom the 20 mm ShVAK cannon was no longer required (the VVa-23 gun was then standard); the quantities of this fine weapon on hand were, therefore, surplus to requirements. On the other hand, examples of the 12.7 mm UBS were scarce-- in fact so much so that surviving MiG-3s often later had these weapons stripped from them and turned over for Yak-7 production! Thus, with ShVAK on hand, and these able to fit comfortably where the UBS had been mounted, the 30 examples of the last MiG variant from Kuibishev were armed with two synchronised 20 mm guns. It is thought that the cowling was unmodified from the last (p/n 4950-5250) series built in Moscow. Additionally, most of these examples, with the curious Production Numbers (6001-6030), seemed to have been completed without a radio mast, and with a fixed tail wheel resembling the later Moscow area field modifications. No information is available on the type(s) of the under wing fittings that may have been installed on these aircraft.

Appendix I: Development of Lengthened Nose From MiG-1 to MiG-3

Throughout the long course of literature regarding the MiG-3 family there has existed much confusion on the matter of over-all fuselage length. It was widely known that the I-200 prototype and the subsequent MiG-1 series featured a length of 8155 mm. The last MiG-3s were also known to have an over-all length of 8250 mm. But, wherein lie the change in length? Clear modifications to the nose of the MiG-3, from the early cowling pattern to the later, created the idea that the nose length must have resulted from these changes. This notion stood unchallenged for years, and indeed even gave rise to the use of the terms "short-nose" and "long-nose" MiG-3.

All of these assumptions were, in fact, spurious. The true picture was uncovered during the course of quite outstanding work by researcher Evgenniy Arsen'ev. It was he who finally realised that the change in length occurred between the MiG-1 and the MiG-3 production versions; a fact subsequently proved with documentation, and later by direct measurements of surviving specimens. The different cowl arrangements on the earlier and later MiG-3s did not instigate a change in length, but they did result in a further change in exhaust stack, a fact which has possibly led to the on-going confusion regarding this topic.

MiG-1 = 8155 mm
MiG-3 = 8250 mm

95 mm   =   55 mm + 40 mm longer spinner

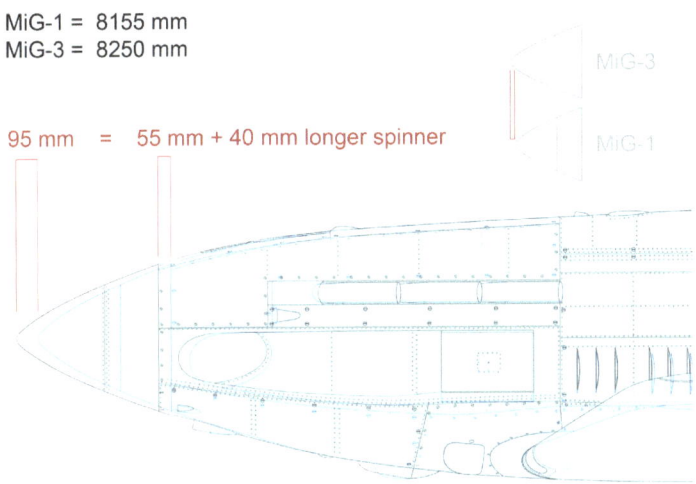

As can be seen above and below, the mounting of the engine and the position of the exhaust stacks was identical.

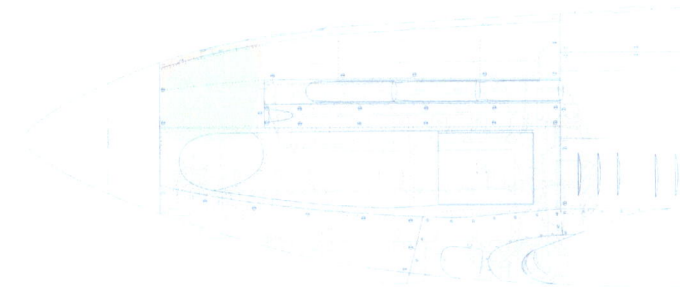

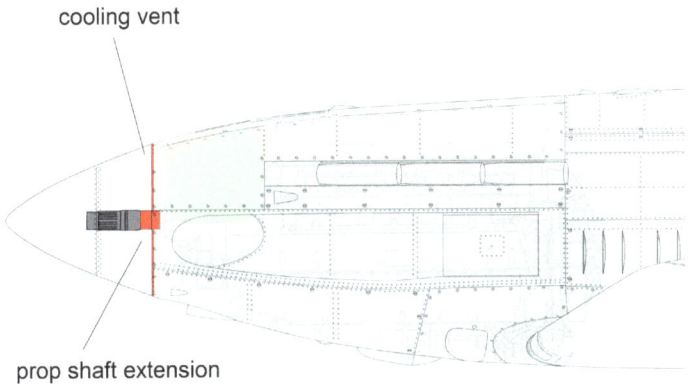

cooling vent

prop shaft extension

[Left] This drawing shows the early pattern MiG-3 nose super-imposed over the original MiG-1 (blue tint). All of the 95 mm difference in length was found at the front of the cowling, in addition to a slightly larger spinner, which was 40 mm longer than the original unit over-all. The MiG-3's nose was extended 55 mm forward, making for less crowded conditions at the front of the engine bay with regards to the oil and coolant header tanks. [Below, Left] A cooling vent was added to the MiG-3's nose in the expanded space, and the propellor shaft was suitably lengthened to fit the new arrangement (*changes shown in red*).

[Above] The tight fit in the nose of the MiG-1 is evident in this image. Note the (missing) two-piece upper cowling unit arrangement.

[Below] Restored MiG-3 p/n 4741 shows the cooling vent plate as seen on the MiG-3. The additional 55 mm extension to the cowling is clearly apparent in this view.

Appendix II: Development of MiG-3 Nose From Early Pattern Cowling (*dzuz fastener*) to Late Style (*latch*)

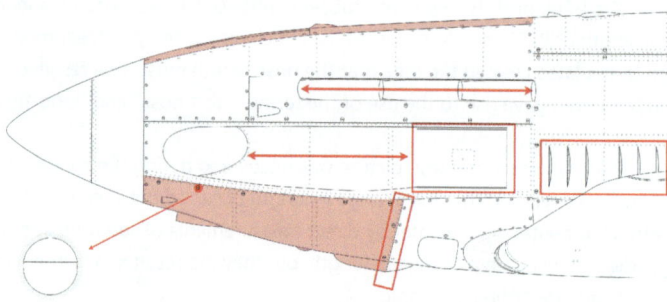

The early MiG-3 cowling with *dzuz* type fasteners [see inset, Left] featured three main pieces (two along the top of the cowl) which were removed for normal maintenance and service (*pink shade*). The oil cooler tunnels were slightly longer than on later types and were followed by six vents aft of the exhaust flap, which featured a small gap surrounding the unit. The exhaust stacks were slightly elongated, and extended just past the main cowling pieces covering the engine. The bottom cowl piece featured a slanted rear face, which when removed left a small portion of the generator cover still in place.

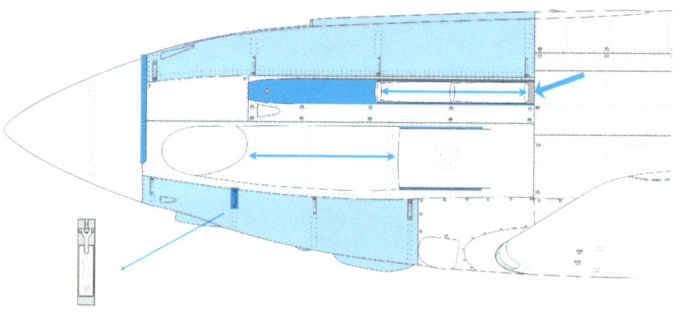

The late MiG-3 cowling with latch type fasteners [see inset, Left] featured two main pieces which were removed for normal maintenance and service (*light blue shade*). The oil cooler tunnels were slightly shorter than on earlier types, and featured triangle shaped guide pieces (top and bottom) for the moveable exit flap. The exhaust stacks were slightly shorter and more rounded with a very large fairing covering the first stack, and terminated just before the main cowling pieces covering the engine (leaving a gap). Access to the engine, as can be seen, was very much improved by the new unit, particularly around the cylinder heads, which are covered on the original cowling type. A small strip was applied to the front of the cowling to keep hydraulic (and other) fluid from blowing back onto the windscreen.

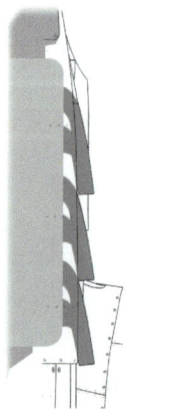 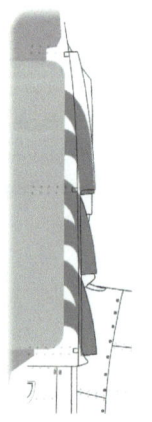

[Left] A cut-away view of the exhaust stacks from the top, with the early pattern cowl to left and the later style to right. The later stacks can be seen to be shorter and more rounded, which explains their location as seen from the side of the nose. No change in the engine's position nor mounting took place during the MiG fighter's production development.

Glossary & Abbreviations

GPW Great Patriotic War, usually refers to the 2nd World War against Nazi Germany, but can be used to refer to the Napoleonic War of 1812

HSU Hero of the Soviet Union, *The Gold Star* medal

IAD (*Istrebitel'nii Aviadiviziya*) Fighter Air Division, usually comprising four to six Regiments

IAK (*Istrebitel'nii Aviakorpus*) Fighter Air Corps, usually comprising three to five Divisions

IAP (*Istrebitel'nii Aviapolk*) Fighter Air Regiment, usually comprising three to four Squadrons

LII (*Letno-Islyedovatel'skii Institut*) Flight Research Institute

NKAP or Narkomaviaprom (*Narodnii Kommissariat Aviatsionoi Promishlinosti*) People's Commissariat for the Aircraft Industry

NII VVS (*Nauchno-Ispitatel'nii Institut Voyenno-Vozdushikh Sil*) Scientific Test Institute of the Army Air Forces

OKB (*Opitnoe Konstruktorskoe Byuro*) Experimental Design Bureau

P/N Production Number, also given frequently in Russian sources as **Factory Number**; the terms are synonymous

Polk (*Aviapolk*) Regiment (Aviation Regiment)

UTI (*Uchebno-trenirovannii istrebitel'*) Fighter-Trainer Aircraft

UVVS (*Upravlenie Voyenno-Vozdushnikh Sili*) Directorate of the Air Forces

VVS (*Voyenno-Vozdushne Sili*) Army Air Forces

VVS VMF (*Voyenno-Vozdushne Sili Voenno-Morskogo Flota*) Naval Air Forces

Cyrillic Transliteration Method

The new Russian to English transliteration system employed in the Profile & Scale series.

Lightning Source UK Ltd.
Milton Keynes UK
UKHW050830230220
359152UK00003B/34